(16)
FUKUMI
(PROTÉGÉ):
?

TONY **HOOD**

author**HOUSE**®

AuthorHouse™
1663 Liberty Drive
Bloomington, IN 47403
www.authorhouse.com
Phone: 1 (800) 839-8640

Published by AuthorHouse 08/13/2018

ISBN: 978-1-5462-5448-5 (sc)
ISBN: 978-1-5462-5447-8 (e)

Print information available on the last page.

This book is printed on acid-free paper.

INTRODUCTION

Terrence Good is a Tennessee native who grew up in a broken home. His step mother (Lynn) split from his father (Harrison Good) who struggles with alcohol addiction. Defiantly, Terrence's popularity as a California high school basketball prospect is cut short when; he walks out on his SAT exam, and his team is knocked out of the first round of the CIF playoffs. His NBA basketball career doesn't pan out and he has to pursue an entry level job. Chad Fukumi is a 35 year old devoted Asian American husband and bright sales agent in a cutthroat electricity firm. He asserts himself as a basketballoholic who is very overprotective of his daughter Candace Fukumi who has the IQ of a rocket scientist. Chad's sidekick Bob, who's overzealous and not afraid to speak his mind, acts as a mediator between the two of them. Terrence struggles to make ends meet and cope in the ninetofive world, he's evicted from his apartment and he's left to sleep in his dysfunctional car in slum neighborhoods in downtown Los Angeles. No longer able to cope with his failure of becoming a professional basketball player, he sells his pride and joy (a profession grade leather basketball given to him by Harrison when he was a kid). This shameful reality brings Terrence depression and guilt. He finds a powerful amateur basketball coach (coach Mayday) who provides him an opportunity to make a good living by training his basketball prospects. He begins pursuing his dream of making it as a basketball trainer. He crosses paths with Chad who propositions him to train Candace, who has been regarded by coach Mayday's association of basketball trainers as an inept prospect. Terrence doesn't think much of girl's basketball. She lacks athleticism, and she's too short at 5 feet. However, Terrence accepts Chad's handsome offer and she becomes his sixteenth protégé and Terence teaches her some stunning basketball skills. But, when a gritty confrontation befalls Terrence involving coach Mayday's highly sought after blue chipper, he quits his job with nowhere to go. He later reunites with his off and on ex-friend, Tina. Eventually Terrence comes to grips with the fact that he has anger management issues. Despite his family troubles when he was a kid, he realizes that Candace has a mysterious talent-gift that stems far beyond the game of basketball, hopeful she will redeem him as a basketball coach.

CHAPTER ONE

TERRENCE GOOD" then
"AGE SIX" LOS ANGELES

EXT. BASKETBALL COURTS - DAY

Terrence good is performing a series of basketball drills with his father Harrison Good (18).

TERRENCE (narrative)
I was just six years of age the first time I picked up a NBA basketball. I wasn't one of those kids who came from a wealthy family nor was I one of those kids who rocked one hundred dollar pair of air Jordan sneakers each time he set foot on the basketball court. However, I was fortunate to have a father take me under his wing and teach me how to play the game — step-by-step.

They say that those who want it bad enough are the same ones who are willing to work hard to achieve their goals day in and day out. At the tender age of six, I was in search of the American Dream, I was in search of the good life — by way of someday being drafted into N.B.A

SENIOR YEAR then APRIL 26 2014 LOS ANGELES

EXT. TERRENCE GOOD HOUSE - DAY: A middle-class neighborhood.

TERRENCE GOOD
NBA, here I come, baby!

TERRENCE GOOD, eighteen years old, intently staring at the tube, sitting next to CARL and DE-ROCK, also eighteen. They are watching the Indiana Pacers vs. Atlanta Hawks, game 4.Terrence — afro, wears a "NBA BOUND" t-shirt.

TERRENCE (cont'd)
All these fans gone be chanting my name...! Terrence..! Terrence..!

CARL
Stone cold, Mr. Terrence Good!

DE-ROCK (to Terrence)
You really think you have a shot?

TERRENCE

We shall see.

CARL (to Terrence)

Bra, you can do anything you set your mind to.

TERRENCE (swagger)

They don't know it yet, but, the real NBA super star is sitting right here — I'm just waiting for my name to be called.

They all laugh. Just then Terrence notices on the tube: "NBA Half Time Report" breaking news "Clipper's Owner Donald Sterling Race Rant!"

CARL (points at tube)

Oh snap, yo' T. Check it out!

Terrence looks at the tube.

TERRENCE (shocked)

This is insane!!!

Terrence stares at the tube, shocked.

CARL

Man, are we ever going to get over this race thing?

TERRENCE

No kidding.

DE-ROCK

Just because you up in the league making millions, don't mean you can't be hated on.

CARL (stares at tube)

Damn shame.

HARRISON (36) and LYNN (32) are arguing from the bedroom. They move into the living room. They stop in front of the tube, still arguing.

LYNN (to Harrison, pissed)

I thought I told you that if I ever caught you cheating on me — it's over between us.

TERRENCE

Mom, do you and dad mind?
We're trying to watch the game here.

LYNN (to Harrison)

Do you love her? The other woman.

HARRISON

I love you more than anything in this world.

LYNN

Oh really?Are you sure about that?

Harrison tries to hug her, she dodges.

LYNN (cont'd)

Then how come I found these tucked down in your sock drawer?

She holds up red silk stockings.

HARRISON

Umm, sweetheart, I got those for you — for that trip we took to Palm Springs last summer, don't you remember?

She turns to Terrence.

LYNN (contd)

Terrence, your daddy is a no-good-lying-cheat.

HARRISON (dispassionately)

Baby, don't bring him into this, please.

CARL (to DE-ROCK, nervously)

I think we should be heading out now.

DE-ROCK (excited)

Forget that, this is getting good.

CARL rushes up, grabs DE-ROCK, they exit. Terrence is embarrassed.

TERRENCE (to HARRISON and LYNN)

I'll be out on the front porch.

Terrence grabs his NBA basketball next to the front door, he exits.

LYNN (pissed)

Harrison Good, I am leaving the country tonight, and don't you dare come looking for me.

HARRISON

Baby, wait....

Lynn tosses silk stockings at Harrison's face. She exits. Harrison just stands there, dejected.

EXT. TERRENCE GOOD HOUSE - DAY: Terrence sits on steps. Lynn runs by Terrence, crying. She stops and turns to Terrence.

LYNN (cont'd)

Terrence, when you become a man someday, take care of your family, provide for them.

She kisses his forehead. She runs off crying. Terrence is sad. Harrison comes up from behind. Terrence rolls his eyes.

HARRISON

Let her leave, It's not like she was your real
mom anyway.

TERRENCE

My real mom would have punched your lights out.

HARRISON

Don't you go believing a word that women says.
She's nothing but trouble.

TERRENCE

Dad, have it ever accrued to you that maybe you're
doing something terribly wrong with the ladies?

HARRISON

Maybe it's time I find you another step mom.

TERRENCE

You see, that's the part I don't get.
You act like these women are a dime a dozen to
you, what gives?

HARRISON

We'll talk about it later.

Harrison gets up, enters house. Terrence looks at NBA logo on his basketball.
He sees a multi-racial group moving down the sidewalk. He stares out. He
looks at his NBA basketball.

TERRENCE

I find it very hard to believe that racism exist in
the NBA. Never say never.

He stares out.

TERRENCE (cont'd)

I'm gonna be the best thing that ever happen to the NBA.

CARL and DE-ROCK return out of breath.

DE-ROCK (to Terrence)

You up for a game of 3 on 3?

TERRENCE

Nah I'm cool. Got way too much on my mind right now.

They stare at him.

TERRENCE

My step mom just walked out on me like I didn't mean nothing to her. Not to mention this mess going down in the NBA.

De-rock walks off.

CARL

Hey man, just let it go....

TERRENCE (cont'd)

It aint that easy for everyone.
This is my career we're talking about.

Carl glances at De-rock off in the distance.

CARL (cont'd)

I'll be down at the courts if you change your mind.

He walks off. Terrence stares at his NBA basketball.

TERRENCE

When I'm out on the court the last thing that
matters to me is the color of another man's skin.
You could be green or purple for all I care.

He glances back at the tube. Shakes his head. He gets up and moves down
the sidewalk, dribbling his NBA basketball. He passes by a basketball gym.
Whistles blowing and Men, Women, and young girls voices. He shoots the
NBA ball in the air!

TERRENCE (cont'd)

...and the crowd goes wild!

EXT. BASKETBALL GYM - CONTINUOUS: A ten years old girl's Asian
Basketball Game. Candace, ten years old, sits at the end of the bench, intently
watching USC women's basketball game on her iPhone — She is impressed
by the Trojan's showmanship. Wears a PHANTOM PRIDE jersey. CHAD,
35, watches her from the stands.

CHAD (to himself)

Honey, pay attention to the game.

Her mother, JANE, 30, walks up to her, holding a water bottle.

JANE

Here's an extra bottle of water in case you want
to share with your friends.

Candace nods. Jane sets the water bottle next to Candace. She moves over
to the stands, sits next to Chad. Chad glances at the scoreboard. Phantom's
down 20.

CHAD (concerned)

Are they ever gonna put her in the game?

JANE

That would be nice.

CHAD

She seems so isolated from the other kids.

JANE

Maybe I should go talk to her.

Candace waves at Chad and Jane. She picks up and drinks from the water bottle. She stares out. Her eyes reveal a cluster of silhouettes moving along the court. The game buzzer rings.

CHAD

Well at least she looks good in her new uniform.

Chad and Jane raise up and begin loudly cheering for Candace.

INT. TERRENCE GOOD HOUSE - BEDROOM - DAY: Terrence lays on his bed in his bedroom, reading a NBA sports magazine. At the door, his girlfriend, TINA, sketches a figure of him, with a pencil, on a large rectangular shaped canvas. She is 18, beautiful. Terrence, lights up at Tina's effort. He laughs.

TERRENCE

I could see you in the Guinness book of world records with that piece. Caption: Terrence The Mighty Basketball God.

Tina looks up, smiles. She goes back to doodling.

TERRENCE (cont'd)

Don't forget about me when you're all big and famous.

Tina laughs out loud.

TINA

You should be the one to talk, Mr. Basketball.

Terrence goes back to reading.

She glances at the magazine.

> ### TINA (cont'd)
> What are you reading?

Terrence scans magazine.

> ### TERENCE
> Nothing that would interest you. Just trying to
> see who they predict to go in the first round of
> the NBA draft this year. Guy stuff.

Tina frowns, tosses pencil at him. Terrence quickly jumps up, and tackles her
down to the ground.

> ### TERRENCE (cont'd)
> Oh you wanna play, what did I tell you about
> starting stuff you know you can't finish.

They playfully roll around on the ground, tickling each other.

> ### TERRENCE (cont'd) (laughing)
> Okay-okay, you win.

They raise up.

> ### TINA
> What am I gonna do when you get drafted into
> the NBA? Because you know what they say, right?

> ### TERRENCE
> No, what do they say?

> ### TINA
> They say that after every road game, there's a
> bus load of groupies who hang out in the hotel
> lobby, preying on incredibly good looking guys
> on the team.

                    TERRENCE

You aint got nothing to worry about because I
plan on having you right there with me.

She stares into his eyes.

                    TINA

That's exactly what I wanted to hear.

                    TERRENCE

When I make it to the NBA, I'm gonna buy you
the most beautiful house in Beverly Hills, white
picket fence, jacuzzi tub, and a butler to wait on
you hand and foot.

                    TINA

...and a poodle?

Terrence laughs.

                    TERRENCE

I'll buy you a thousand poodles.

                    TINA

Oh baby, I love you so much.

She hugs him, she kisses him on the cheek.

She looks down at her watch.

            TINA (concerned) (cont'd)

Oh shoot, I'm late for my art class.

She rushes up.

            TERRENCE (sarcastically)

Yeah, okay, that's way more important than
spending some quality time with your man.

TINA

Terrence, come on, if I don't maintain a 4.0 GPA Yale will pull my art scholarship right from underneath my nose.

TERRENCE

Baby, now you know I'm kidding, of course I want you to get accepted into Yale.

She half-smiles, grabs her backpack and coat.

TINA

How are you doing on your SAT preps?

                    TERRENCE

Fair.

She gives him a strange look.

                      TINA

Remember what we talked about — you need to
dedicate at least two hours a day in your study
group.

                    TERRENCE

I know-I know...I got it covered.

She kisses him on his cheek.

                      TINA

I'll see you later today.

She exits. Terrence signs.

EXT. PLAYGROUND - COURTS - DAY: Chad stands next to a generic
basketball hoop giving Candace a shooting lesson. Candace stands a few feet
away from Chad AWKWARDLY holding a rubber basketball.

              CHAD (mimes shooting)

Keep both eyes on the ball.

Candace mimes Chad's instructions.

                CHAD (cont'd)

Nice and easy....

She THROWS up a shot. The ball HITS Chad on his shoulder, he GRABS
his shoulder in discomfort.

                CHAD (cont'd)

Ouch! You're suppose to aim for the basket!

CANDACE (makes gestures)
I did!

CHAD
Do you think the USC coach is gonna recruit you
if you keep doing that crap?

She gestures: "I don't know"

INT. GYM - CONTINUOUS: Terrence goes through a routine workout by
himself. He takes a couple shots, grabs the rebound and repeats.

TERRENCE
All or none baby!

He sinks a couple of three pointers. He runs over to the sideline. Picks up the
NBA magazine. Scans the magazine.

TERRENCE (cont'd)
Drill number twenty five!

He sets down the magazine, runs back over to the court, does tricks with the
basketball. He is serious. He is on a mission.

TERRENCE (cont'd)
Five seconds left, the ball goes into, GOOD.

He flips the ball to himself. He catches the ball. He sinks a jumper.

TERRENCE (cont'd)
Bottom of the net!

The Playground: Chad runs over by the hoop, picks up the ball and HANDS
it back to Candace.

CHAD
Try again.

She throws up a shot again. Nothing but air! Chad gets frustrated. He walks up to her.

CHAD (bothered) (cont'd)

Is...everything okay?

CANDACE

Dad, I don't think my coach likes me one bit.

CHAD

Why sure your coach likes you, why else would your coach let you play on the team if he didn't like you?

CANDACE

...But I never get to play in any of the games.

CHAD

If you wanna see playing time you have to keep practicing.

Candace looks down, sad.

CHAD (cont'd)

Why else do you think we're out here practicing all this stuff?

Candace shrugs her shoulders.

CHAD (cont'd)

Okay, I got it, you know how your teacher assigns you homework a couple days before you have a really big test?

Candace quickly nods.

CHAD (cont'd)

Good, now hold that thought.

Candace scratches her head, unsure.

                    CANDACE
I still don't understand.

                     CHAD
The reason why you finish your homework every
single night, is because?

                    CANDACE
....Because, you and mom make me?

                     CHAD
No.

Candace is unsure. She glances at a AFRICAN AMERICAN MALE and
a CAUCASIAN MALE playing one on one, at the other end of the court.
She sees things in a silhouette — of both men playing an intense game of one
on one.

                CHAD (cont'd)
I'm running out of ideas here...

Candace continues to stare at the men.

                CHAD (cont'd)
Okay. Do you remember the time your mother
had that really important state exam for dental
school?

Candace is oblivious. Continues to stare at the men....She slowly nods.

                CHAD (cont'd)
Great! Now, just try to imagine what would of
happened if your mother would have, simply-sort
of-blew off her studies.

The two men high five each other. Candace stares at them.

Chad snaps his fingers, tries to get her attention.

CHAD (cont'd)
Candace, look at me when I'm talking to you.

CANDACE
Yeah dad, I heard you the first time...

CHAD
Just great. Now will you please answer the question.

CANDACE (looks at Chad)
I guess what you're trying to say is that I should practice as hard as mom did when she was in dental school, so that I can reap the benefits of our dental care plan in case I get my teeth knocked out in the game — that's if I ever get chance to play.

CHAD

Umm, okay, works for me...

Basketball Gym: Terrence is drenched in sweat. He stands at the free throw line. He shoots. Swish!

Harrison peeks inside the gym. Sees Terrence. He is impressed. Terrence runs suicides.

HARRISON

There's nothing more entertaining then cutting in on a man who takes his job serious.

Terrence looks at Harrison. He goes through a routine ball handling drill.

HARRISON (cont'd)

I got a call in today from a division two contender who might be interested in signing you on a full ride. They wanted to know if you had committed to anyone yet. I told them that you were still weighing out all your options.

Terrence slam dunks the basketball, hard. He moves over to Harrison.

TERRENCE

Did they say anything else?

HARRISON

It was just an inquiry.

TERRENCE

Dad, I already told you what my plans are, did you forget?

HARRISON

The NBA, for the thousand time.

TERRENCE

I won't settle for anything less.

HARRISON (cont'd)

Relax, they're a division two contender. Worst case scenario.

TERRENCE

What about their offense, did they say if they run the flex offense or not?

HARRISON

I didn't ask.

TERRENCE

Come on pops, I thought you were in my corner.

Terrence gets upset, throws down the basketball, moves over to the stance.

HARRISON

Terrence, I'll do everything in my power to help delay the process of you becoming academically eligible, but son, I'm not your agent...

Terrence nods.

HARRISON (cont'd)

Anyway, there's a three day sale going on at one of my favorite Italian suit outlets in North Hollywood, so I thought that maybe after your workout we could head over there and pick you out a suit for your high school graduation.

Terrence happily nods.

HARRISON (cont'd)

Meet me out front when you're done.

He walks off. Terrence is excited.

INT. CANDACE HOUSE - DINING ROOM - NIGHT: Candace stands with her back against the dining room wall. Chad stands next to her holding a ruler as he measures her growth. Jane and Melissa sit at the table eating dinner and watching them both.

> ### CANDACE (to Chad)
> Am I gonna turn heads?

Chad sets the ruler over Candace's head.

> ### CANDACE (cont'd)
> Well!Am I?!Am I?! How's it looking?

Chad is still measuring.

> ### CHAD
> ...Umm, not quite, you still have a little ways to go sweetie...

Candace gets frustrated, tries to leave, Chad yanks her back as Melissa giggles. Candace glances up at the ruler.

> ### CANDACE (dispassionately)
> I'm gonna be this size forever.

> ### CHAD
> You're gonna grow sweetie, you just have to be patient.

Candace angrily SNATCHES the ruler and tosses it. Chad gives her a look. They both sit at the table. Candace sulks.

> ### JANE (to Candace)
> Candace, your dinner's getting cold.

> ### CANDACE
> But it's not fair.

Jane signs...

                    CHAD (to Jane)
I've been thinking about having a man-to-man
with Candace's basketball coach.

                    JANE
About what?

                    CHAD
About the fact that we're not paying that program
just so we can watch our daughter ride the pine.

                    JANE
It's your call.

                    CHAD
It's important for Candace to understand that
there are no "I's" in team.

                    JANE
Well, I would only hope that Candace's coach
had a very good explanation for why he doesn't
play her.

                    CHAD
I can think of one, how about Candace's coach is
a: big fat zero.

                    JANE
Chad, your tone?

                    CHAD
Oh wait, how about this: What very good
explanation could possibly come from someone
who's not being fair to our daughter?! Just the
thought of it alone sickens me.

JANE (slams down her fork, irritated)

Do we have to do this right now?
Is it possible for once we could sit at the dinner table without having to discuss basketball?

CHAD (stern)

Fine.

JANE (looks up at ceiling)

It's a miracle.

CHAD (looks at Candace)

If this keeps up, we'll just have to find Candace another team, right honey?

Candace approves.

CHAD (cont'd)

New team. New coach.

INT. TERRENCE HOUSE - TERRENCE'S ROOM - CONTINUOUS:
Terrence lays on his bed in his bedroom, eyes wide open. His basketball sits next to him. Harrison enters...

HARRISON (jokily)

Looks like you and your new basketball have already made it to second base — sorry I forgot to knock.

Terrence smiles.

TERRENCE

It's the best present a father could ever give to his son.

Harrison glances at Terrence's Italian suit hanging up on the closet door. Terrence looks at the suit also. He smiles. He raises up, moves over to Harrison, they hug.

                    TERRENCE (cont'd)
Thanks pop.

                    HARRISON
Just promise me one thing.

                    TERRENCE
You name it.

Harrison stares at him.

                    HARRISON
Son, no matter what happens with your dream of
becoming a professional ball player.

Terrence stares...

                    HARRISON (cont'd)
You make sure you get your degree.

Terrence nods.

                    TERRENCE
Okay.

                    HARRISON (proud)
Alright.

He pats Terrence over his shoulder. He exits. Terrence gets back into his bed.
He hugs his basketball.

                    TERRENCE
Basketball is my life.

INT. BASKETBALL GYM - LATE AFTERNOON: Chad rest his back
against the gym door — waiting for the Phantom's to exit the gym. Just then,
the gym door opens — players and parents scatter from inside the gym.
Candace walks up to Chad.

Terrence's Bathroom. Terrence snatches the note off the mirror, he begins to read the note:

"Dear Son, I hope this letter finds you well. There's a few things I'd like to explain.....First, is that, when a woman tells you not to go chasing after her, what she really means is to do the exact opposite....

Terrence sighs.

Basketball Gym again: Chad looks down at Candace.

CHAD

How'd it go in there?

Candace slowly shakes her head, unhappy.

CANDACE (sad)

My coach told me I wasn't tall enough to play for him anymore.

CHAD (cont'd)

That bad huh?

Candace slowly nods, fights back tears. Candace's coach emerges from the gym. Chad sees him. Chad looks down at Candace.

CHAD (cont'd) (serious)

I think I'm gonna have that talk with your coach now.

Candace nervously shakes her head. Chad nods than moves over to coach Mayday.

Chad slowly walks up to coach Mayday.

CHAD

Excuse me coach, do you mind if we have a little chat off to the side.

Chad pulls coach Mayday over to the other side of the gym. Both Chad and coach Mayday glance at Candace.

                    CHAD (cont'd)
That's my daughter, Candace, and well, she just told me that you cut her from your team due to a height restriction.

                    MAYDAY
Not that it's any of your business who I decide to keep on my roaster but, if you must know — in moving forward, yes, I told your daughter that she's too short to play for me.

Chad grows angry. Candace is eavesdropping –looks very sad.

                    MAYDAY (cont'd)
I build champions who are more than likely capable of playing on a division one roster at some point of their basketball career so instead of you being overprotective of your daughter and coming at me with this nonsense you should try a little harder to understand how the process works.

                    CHAD
You haven't given her a fair shot, she's the first one to show up to all your practices and she's always the last one to leave all your practices. Doesn't that count for something?

                    MAYDAY
I'm starting to get the feeling that you thought you could just walk over here and somehow persuade me into changing my mind about keeping your daughter on my team.

Chad is silent.

MAYDAY (cont'd)

It doesn't work that way, this is my team and everyone must play by my rules. Parents included.

He walks away, Chad rushes up from behind, aggressively pushes him up against the wall.

CHAD (cont'd)(aggressively)

I don't ever want to see your face again, scumbag!

CHAD CLENCHES HIS FIST. Coach Mayday is bothered.

MAYDAY

Easy there guy.

He yanks away and walks off.

MAYDAY (cont'd)

Freak!

He exits the gym.

EXT. BASKETBALL COURTS -CONTINUOUS: Terrence goes through a intense routine ball handling drill.

INT. CHAD'S SUV - CONTINUOUS: Chad steers at the wheel, Candace sits, they pass by the playground. Candace sees Terrence-in-action. She is amazed at his showmanship.

EXT. BASKETBALL COURTS -CONTINUOUS: Terrence finishes off a shooting drill and exits the playground.

INT. TERRENCE HOUSE/BATHROOM - CONTINUOUS: Terrence exits the bathroom, moves pass the kitchen, sees Harrison sitting at the dinner table next to two bottles of booze, one of the bottles is half empty, the other is full. Harrison sits holding a glass of booze filled to the brim as he stares at a photo of him and Lynn holding hands. Terrence walks up to him.

TERRENCE

Hey dad, you okay?

HARRISON (Half-drunken)

You know, I've been sitting here thinking to myself, about your chances of turning pro, statics wise that is.

Terrence is confused.

HARRISON (cont'd)(Half-drunken)

Son, after heavy consideration. The odds are not in your favor.

TERRENCE

Dad, what the hell are you talking about? You were the one who said you believed I had a shot at making it to the N.B.A. in the first place. So where is this coming from.

Terrence glances at the bottle of booze and photo of Lynn.

TERRENCE (cont'd)

Never mind, I think I just answered my question.

HARRISON (Half-drunken)

Son, I was just saying what any loving and caring father should say to his son —who's trying to pursue his dream of turning pro. No offense.

TERRENCE

None taken. Dream killer.

He angrily walks off...

"CITY SECTION PLAYOFFS"

EXT. BASKETBALL GYM, LOCKER ROOM -LATE AFTERNOON:
Terrence and his team mates sit in the middle of steel lockers as they listen to coach Miller as he lectures them all. Terrence is in deep thought about Harrison's absence.

EXT. BASKETBALL GYM, LOCKER ROOM - CONTINUOUS:
Terrence drives in for a lay up, his shot is blocked by the opponent. Terrence dribbles up the court and the ball is stolen by the opponent. We see a N.BA. scout sitting in the stance. Terrence shoots a jumper and his shot is blocked by the opponent. Terrence plays defense and is knocked to the ground by the opponent.

He glances in the stance at the N.B.A. scout, then sees Harrison's seat empty.

He gets up and walks off the court. His coach yells at him to continue play.

COACH MILLER (yelling)
Terrence, come back here...!

TERRENCE (angry)
I quit!

He exits the gym, everyone is shocked.

EXT. BASKETBALL GYM, LOCKER ROOM - CONTINUOUS:
Terrence stands in front of his locker, pulls out a gym bag and a bottle of booze. He shoves the bottle in his gym bag and exits.

EXT. STREET -CONTINUOUS: Terrence moves down the street, drinks booze.

EXT. GRAVEYARD -CONTINUOUS: Terrence moves through the graveyard holding bottle of booze. He stops in front of his mother's tombstone, it reads "Joyce M. Good.

TERRENCE

It's been a long time, mom. Now I understand clearly why you kept a lot of thing about the real world away from me. So that I would remain hopeful.

He chugs booze. He looks up at the sky, he starts crying. He squats down in front of Joyce's tombstone. He kisses her tombstone.

TERRENCE

I'm sorry I let you down mom. No one will ever replace you.

He walks off.

INT. TERRENCE'S ROOM - CONTINUOUS: Terrence enters. He heads straight for his SAT prep book sitting on his desk.

He angrily grabs it, and tosses it in the trash can. Out of pure frustration:

He angrily picks up a chair and throws it against the wall. Fatigued. He falls down on his bed. He starts crying...

Tina appears in the doorway.

TINA (concerned)

Terrence what's going on? Your coach just told me that you quit the team.

TERRENCE (sad)

Everyone in my family has walked out on me.

He hands her the letter from Harrison, she reads it, looks up at him.

TINA (soft)

Ooooh baby, you know I would never leave you.

TERRENCE

I don't plan on going to college anymore. This whole idea of me making it to the NBA is starting to sound a little ridiculous.

TINA

Oh, so now I get it — so when the going gets rough you just give up huh? Terrence, are you also telling me that you've given up on us as well?

Terrence is silent.

TINA (cont'd)

Okay, whooo, reality check. This is crazy. I am really disappointed in you, especially after all we have been through.

TERRENCE

I don't need anyone.

TINA (watery eyes)

Is that what you really want?

Tina fights back tears.

TINA (cont'd)

Call me when you're ready to talk, okay.

She moves over to the door, GRABS art sketch of Terrence and exits.

"GRADUATION DAY"

EXT. HIGH SCHOOL, FOOTBALL FIELD – DAY: The sun is high in the sky. Different congratulations banners are posted up on the fences and trees next to the football field. One hundred students wear caps and gowns. They all sit in fold-out chairs scattered throughout the football field watching a woman giving a speech — standing at a podium facing them. Terrence looks down at the ground, in deep thought.

WOMEN (shouts)
Congratulations to the class of two thousand and fourteen!

This is when all the students stand up and start celebrating and throwing their caps and tassels in the air. Terrence just sits there, isolated. Carl and De-rock walk up to him.

TERRENCE (sad)
My own dad don't even care about me anymore.

Terrence remains still, Carl sits next to him and comforts him.

CHAPTER TWO

"THREE MONTHS LATER"

INT. TERRENCE APARTMENT - LATE DAY: A toilet FLUSHING. He emerges from his bathroom. Wears a tightly fitted "MEXICAN-FIESTA" uniform, he grabs and pulls on his uniform in discomfort.

INT. TERRENCE SEDAN – CONTINUOUS: Terrence puts the key in the ignition, pulls off...

INT. RESTAURANT - CONTINUOUS: The inside of the restaurant has a Mexican American theme.

INT. KITCHEN - CONTINUOUS: Terrence walks by TWO CO-WORKERS washing dishes at a nearby sink. He approaches six medium size lockers — he goes to the last locker which is covered in professional basketball teams stickers. He OPENS his locker, we see a huge sticker in the middle of his locker, it reads: "FOLLOW YOUR DREAMS". His boss appears to his left, Mr. Santana, HISPANIC MALE (40)

MR. SANTANA

How do you like the new uniform, Terrence?

TERRENCE (stretches his shirt collar)

It is what it is..

MR. SANTANA

I need you to cover for Marco, apparently his mother is ill again.

Terrence glances at a sink STACKED full of dishes, looks at Mr. Santana, sighs.

TERRENCE

Mr. Santana, this is the third time this week Marco has called off.

MR. SANTANA (makes gestures)

What do you want me to do?

Pissed. He heads toward the sink, GRABS an apron off a rack. Begins scrubbing pots and pans.

MR. SANTANA (cont'd)

I knew I could count on you.

He walks off.

INT. MEXICAN RESTAURANT - NIGHT: Terrence, still busting suds, stands slumped in front of the sink, sweaty. He glances up at the clock. It's midnight! His co-worker clocks out. He finally finishes off the last pot, tosses his apron in the sink, fatigued.

INT. TERRENCE SEDAN/COURTS - CONTINUOUS: He pulls up next to playground, shuts off car, stares out. He sees a multi-cultural group of ballers playing an intense game of 5 on 5. He lights up. He heads over to them...

EXT. BASKETBALL COURTS - CONTINUOUS: He watches from the sideline, HOLDING his NBA basketball — gift from Harrison, still wears his work uniform. A TALL AFRICAN AMERICAN MALE JOCK stops next to him.

MALE JOCK

I got next game!

TERRENCE

It's late, aint you got a wife and kid at home?

MALE JOCK

Not no more, I'm divorced, how about yourself?

TERRENCE

Me and my lady split up a while back.

MALE JOCK

Sorry to hear.

He looks at Terrence's ball.

MALE JOCK (cont'd)

You wanna run next with me?

TERRENCE

Who, me?

MALE JOCK

Yeah, you.

TERRENCE

Thanks, but I gotta be at work before the crack of dawn.

MALE JOCK

What do you do for a living?

TERRENCE

You don't wanna know...

MALE JOCK (jokily)

Well, since you put it that way, never mine..

TERRENCE

What I meant to say was I guess I'm just too embarrassed to talk about it considering I had dreams of playing pro ball.

Terrence CLUTCHES his ball.

                    MALE JOCK
Yeah well, you and everyone else out here.

                    TERRENCE
I'm a dishwasher over at the Mexican Fiesta.
What about you? What's your story?

                    MALE JOCK
I work down at the mill. I blew out my knee my
sophomore year in college.

Terrence glances at a huge brace wrapped around his knee.

                MALE JOCK (cont'd)
Playing ball out here a couple days out of the week
is as good as it's gonna get for me.

He walks offs...

                    TERRENCE
I didn't get your name!

                    MALE JOCK
Williams!

                    TERRENCE
Alright, I'll catch you later!

Terrence heads back to his car, gets inside, pulls off...

INT. TERRENCE APARTMENT/HALLWAY - DAY: Terrence OPENS
HIS MAILBOX, pulls out a cluster of mail pieces and a "RENT PAST DUE"
note sitting on top of his mail. He also SEES a letter addressed from Harrison.
He shuts mailbox, moves down the hallway. Just then, he TRIPS over a small
child sitting in the middle of the hallway. The kids gets up, runs off, leaves
behind a clipboard, Terrence SEES it, PICKS IT UP.

TERRENCE (shouts)

Hey kid! You forgot your clipboard!

INT. TERRENCE APARTMENT/STUDIO -CONTINUOUS: He moves over to the tube in the living room, turns on tube, sits on a plush leather couch.... FLIPS channels...sees a variety of different news topics discussing "RACE RELATIONS"....FLIPS channels again, sees AFRICAN AMERICAN comedian DL HUGHLEY.

DL HUGHLEY states:

"BLACK PEOPLE SHOULD AUTOMATICALLY GET TO GO TO HEAVEN BECAUSE WE ALREADY BEEN THROUGH HELL".

Terrence LAUGHS...then looks down at his coffee table, SCANS different ethnic magazines sitting on the table, he moves over to the kitchen, OPENS the frig, pulls out a bucket of KFC chicken. He raises up TWO DRUMSTICKS.

TERRENCE

White or dark meat?

He CHUMPS off a piece of the dark meat drumstick. He tosses the bucket of chicken back in the frig. He grabs a coke. He moves back over to the couch, sits, continues flipping channels. Just then, a knock on the door...

TERRENCE

Who is it?!

MALE VOICE

Manager!

He gets up, moves over to door, opens door. A CAUCASIAN MALE appears.

MANAGER

Terrence, your rent is still two months past due.

TERRENCE

Mr. Smith, how many times do we have to go through this?

MANAGER

As many times as it takes.

He glances at Terrence's television.

MANAGER (cont'd)

I see your cable bill has been paid on time. Priorities...priorities...

TERRENCE

I gotta have my sports.

The manager shows a blank stare.

TERRENCE

Are you insinuating that I'm trying to get over on you?

MANAGER

Possibly, yes.

TERRENCE

Mr Smith, with all due respect. I'm just trying to keep my head above water. Can you feel my pain?

He just stares at Terrence. Terrence looks him up and down.

TERRENCE (cont'd)

I didn't think so.

MANAGER

That wasn't necessary.

TERRENCE (frustrated)

Look, my boss keeps cutting my hours at work but the good news is that I've been looking for a second job.

MANAGER

Terrence, cut the BS, two more weeks and that's it...

Just before he can complete his sentence Terrence rudely SLAMS the door in his face.

MANAGER (cont'd)

Pay your rent or get out!

TERRENCE (upset)

Whatever!!!

He spits at the door.

TERRENCE (cont'd)

You people think you own everything.

He moves back over to the couch, takes a load off. THREE FIRM KNOCKS on the door. He sighs.

TERRENCE (firm)

I'm not here.

CARL

It's me, Carl!

He gets up, moves over to the door again. Carl is twenty, wears Louise Vuitton threads. Carl enters. They both move back over to the couch.

CARL (buddy hug)

Man I've been looking all over for you, where you been hiding?

TERRENCE (sarcastically)

I work for a living.

CARL (offended)

What are you trying to say?

Terrence stares at his threads.

TERRENCE

I think I'm saying it.

CARL

Don't hate the playa hate the game.

TERRENCE

All I know is that if my grandfather left me a huge inheritance to where I could retire like yesterday, I'd probably be sitting around all day playing XBOX my damn self, everybody aint able to be young millionaires.

Carl picks up remote control, flips channels...

CARL

Anything good on TV?

TERRENCE

Same old crap.

CARL

You know I'm having my twenty first birthday party in the Hamptons, right?

TERRENCE

Nah I didn't, you doing it like that?

                              CARL

You know it! You're welcome to come. I'm
thinking about enforcing a dress code and a one
drink minimum per guest.

                           TERRENCE

Hold up, you want me to fly all the way out to the
Hamptons just to celebrate your birthday?

                              CARL

Yeah, why is there a problem?

                           TERRENCE

...And just how am I suppose to get out there?
You gone lend me your private jet?

                              CARL

Let me get back to you on that.

Carl watches NBA basketball on the tube.

                           TERRENCE

When's the last time you heard from De-rock?

                              CARL

About a week ago.

                           TERRENCE

What's he up to?

                              CARL

...Moved to Atlanta to pursue his music career.

                           TERRENCE

Why am I not surprised..

Terrence stares at the tube intently. Carl notices him.

CARL

You thinking about making another run at the NBA?

Terrence has a flashback: On the basketball court, Terrence makes several jumpers. Terrence blocks an opposing team members attempt for a lay up. Terrence does fancy tricks with the basketball pass TWO DEFENDERS. The crowd goes nuts.

LIVING ROOM:

TERRENCE (sighs)

Not with my work schedule — it's bad enough that my landlord is on my back about his last two months rent I owe him, you wouldn't happened to have a couple hundred laying around that you could loan me would you?

Carl reaches in his pants pocket, pulls out a roll of money, hands it all to Terrence. Terrence light up.

TERRENCE (shocked)

Aw man, this helps out a lot, I promise I'll pay you back — it may take me a minute — but you know I'm good for it.

They bump fists.

CARL

Bros gotta look out for each other.

They just sit there and watch the tube together.

INT. MEXICAN RESTAURANT - NIGHT: Terrence stands at the sink, sweaty, busting suds. He glances up at temperature gauge. Temperature Gauge close: 90 degrees. Mr. Santana appears...

MR. SANTANA

Terrence, were getting backed up out there, I need you to move a little faster.

TERRENCE

I'm going as fast as I can, I only got two arms.

MR SANTANA

I need servings set for two more bar mitzvahs in less than an hour.

TERRENCE

I'm on it.

He exits. Terrence starts busting suds at a rapid pace. He stacks plates about three feet tall and moves them next to FOUR CHEFS.

TERRENCE

These should hold you over for now..

He quickly moves back over to sink, starts on pots and pans. He scrubs the pots and pans hard, stacks them on top of each other, moves next to chefs again.

TERRENCE (cont'd)

In coming.

He rushes back over to the sink, this would be when Mr. Santana enters the kitchen holding a stack of dirty plates, sets them next to Terrence.

TERRENCE (cont'd) (shocked)

There must be over a hundred people here tonight.

Mr Santana pats him on the back, walks off. Terrence moves over to dining room entrance, PEEKS out the kitchen door, SEES one hundred Jewish men, women, and children, partying, laughing, dancing. They are having a blast.

TERRENCE (cont'd)
Must be nice.

He moves back over to sink, continues scrubbing, plates, pots and pans.

EXT. MEXICAN RESTAURANT/ PATIO - NIGHT: Terrence sits on the ground while sipping a coke. His face is worn. He holds his basketball. He sets down his coke and begin doing fancy tricks with his ball as he lets off some steam. This would be when Chad's SUV moves pass Terrence.

INT. CHAD'S SUV — CONTINUOUS: Candace sits in the passenger seat, sees Terrence-in-action, she is wide eyed and amazed at his show man ship...They move down the street. Terrence continues his dribbling exhibition. He stops and sits down.

A TEENAGE CAUCASIAN GROUP pass by, they all look at him. He snaps at them.

TERRENCE
What are you looking at?! You got a staring problem?! Hard working black man can't relax on his lunch break?!

They nervously run off. He sees a CAUCASIAN WOMEN walking her dog. He TOSSES the coke at her. She dodges it.

TERRENCE (cont'd)
You think just because you got a cute little pooch that you're better than me?!

CAUCASIAN WOMEN
That can almost hit me, loser!!!

HE RAISES UP, she joggles away fearing for her life.

TERRENCE (cont'd)
Yeah, that's what I thought...

Mr. Santana walks up from behind.

MR. SANTANA (disappointedly)
Terrence, what has gotten into you?

Terrence is caught off guard, he rushes up to face Mr. Santana.

TERRENCE
Umm, Mr. Santana, how long have you been standing there?

MR SANTANA (stern)
Long enough.

TERRENCE
Umm-umm, these kids were making horrible remarks about my uniform and then this old lady kept nagging me about her dog being sick and I lost my cool.

MR SANTANA
Terrence, I saw the whole thing,

TERRENCE
Look, I messed up, aright.

MR. SANTANA
Terrence, I can't have this type of behavior in my establishment.

TERRENCE
Mr. Santana, It won't happen again I promise.

MR SANTANA
Terrence, you're a damn good worker, however, I'm gonna have to ask you to turn over your badge and uniform.

TERRENCE

Mr. Santana, nooooo, please, I really need this job, please understand.

MR. SANTANA

Terrence, hand over your badge and uniform right now!

Terrence is upset, he begins removing his uniform, he strips down to his boxers and t shirt. He HANDS it to Mr. Santana.

MR. SANTANA

Get help.

Mr. Santana enters restaurant, SLAMS door. Terrence's face is tight, moves over to his car, gets inside. He nervously stares at different people passing by.

He looks in his rear view mirror.

TERRENCE

I've become my worst enemy. A judgmental bigot.

He TURNS ON THE RADIO. We hear the DJ discussing a third world country racially charged war. He begins gently caressing his bronze skin tone: face, arms and neck. HE RUBS HIS FINGERS THROUGH HIS NAPPY HAIR, continues listening to the radio. He nervously looks around again. He is a wreck, he beats the steering wheel, frantically.

TERRENCE (angry)

No!!! No!!! No!!! No!!! This can't be happening.

He PICKS UP A BOTTLE OF BOOZE sitting in the back seat, UNSCREWS LID, CHUGS...He quickly starts up car, pulls of...

INT. TERRENCE SEDAN/COURTS - CONTINUOUS: Terrence gets out of car holding his NBA basketball and booze — still in his boxers and under tee. He sees an intense game of 5 on 5...moves over to the court... He sees an AFRICAN AMERICAN JOCK (21) — Terrence's high school teammate.

He is training a CAUCASIAN KID (6). Terrence passes by them both.

AFRICAN AMERICAN JOCK
Long time, Terrence. Good to see you man!

TERRENCE
Hey Antonio, how's life?

AFRICAN AMERICAN JOCK
Can't complain.

TERRENCE
Who's your friend?

AFRICAN AMERICAN JOCK
His name is, Jack! Best known for his "ball hawk" capability.

TERRENCE
Yeah, well, you stay on him..

AFRICAN AMERICAN JOCK
I'm still your biggest fan! Hamilton high vs. Mercy high, you remember don't you? We were down by fifteen at the half — you brought us back man –that's one game I'll never forget..

Terrence CHUGS booze..

AFRICAN AMERICAN JOCK
That bottle aint gone get you nowhere. You use to be the man, T.

FLASHBACK: Mercy High vs. Hamilton High. A raucous crowd. Terrence is in the huddle... his teammates smell defeat... Terrence sinks several jumpers putting his team in striking distance... He steals the ball with three second left....He pulls for a jumper at the buzzer. Swish! The crowd excitedly rushes the floor, his teammates cheerily lift him up over their shoulders and celebrate. Terrence comes out of his daydream:

TERRENCE

I'm still the man.

He stops at the sideline. He recognizes Williams on court.

TERRENCE (cont'd)

Way-to-go-Williams!

He CHUGS BOOZE....A very physical game, different players are pushing, shoving, and trash talking... half drunken, Terrence edges Williams on as he overachieves all the other players... his would be when William's man makes a dirty play on him, causing a injury to William's rehabilitated knee. Terrence tries to defuse scuffle by moving in between Williams and his man. Terrence gets up in William's mans face.

TERRENCE (mad)

If you got a problem with him, you got a problem with me.

WILLIAMS MAN (makes gestures

Do something about it.

MALE JOCK (To Williams man)

Hey yo man chill out that's Harrison son, my-man is fresh out of rehab.

Terrence walks up to the male jock.

TERRENCE

You think that's funny?

Terrence shoves him back, several players defuse the scuffle. Terrence moves over to Williams and helps him off the court, Williams sits at the sideline rubbing his knee.

WILLIAMS TEAMMATE

We need a sub.

Just then, A TALL AFRICAN AMERICAN MALE walks on the court.

AFRICAN AMERICAN MALE

I can take his spot.

He runs on the court and the game continues... Terrence stares at Williams as he grimace in pain. Candace sees the ordeal from a far as she trains with Chad. She stares at Terrence. Chad watches her.

CHAD

Candace, what are you staring at over there?

CANDACE (excited)

Dad, that's the man I saw the other night when we were leaving the playground. He's got game!

She immediately runs over to Terrence.

CHAD (shouts)

Candace wait!

Candace walks up to Terrence.

CANDACE (soft)

Excuse me sir, is your friend gonna be okay?

TERRENCE

I hope so.

CANDACE

He took a pretty nasty fall.

TERRENCE

He sure did.

Candace stares and as a result, William's skin color turns into a silhouette. Terrence looks around...

                    TERRENCE (cont'd)
          Hey where are your parents?
          You're not here by yourself are you?

                    CANDACE
          I'm here with my dad.

Terrence looks around again, sees Chad.

                    TERRENCE
          Is that him over there?

She glances at Chad. She nods.

                    CANDACE
          My dad and I come here once a week to work on a
          few things, he really thinks I have a shot at playing
          in college someday.

                    TERRENCE
          You play ball?

She happily nods.

                    TERRENCE (cont'd)
          No way, what position?

                    CANDACE
          Guard.

                    TERRENCE
          Hum, I played guard in high school.

He CHUGS BOOZE.

CANDACE

Maybe you can talk to my dad about giving me some pointers.

TERRENCE

Wait-a-sec, I didn't say I was a coach.

CANDACE

Oh, well that's too bad.

Chad runs up to them both.

CHAD

Candace, you can't just run off like that while we are in the middle of our session.

CANDACE

But he's really good dad.

Candace looks at Terrence.

CHAD

I'm sorry, we were going through our weekly routine and she ran over here to meet you.

TERRENCE

It's alright, she's a bright kid.

CHAD (jokily)

She gets it from her mom, of course.

He clasps Terrence's hand.

TERRENCE

My name is, Terrence Good.

CHAD

It's a pleasure to meet you, Terrence.

> **TERRENCE**
>
> Likewise.

> **CANDACE**
>
> Dad, me and Terrence play the same position, maybe he can help me out with some pointers.

> **CHAD**
>
> Is that true, Terrence?

> **TERRENCE**
>
> Yes it's true, but I'm in no position to coach your daughter and besides, you seem to have everything under control.

> **CHAD**
>
> Actually...

Chad slowly shakes his head. Candace frowns.

> **TERRENCE**
>
> I've had a really long day and if you don't mind I'd like to be on my way home now.

HE CHUGS BOOZE. Chad reaches in his pants pocket, pulls out his business card.

> **CHAD**
>
> Here's my card, call me on my cell if you wanna work something out.

Chad hands him his business card.

> **CHAD (cont'd)**
>
> We hope to see you around.

They walk off. Terrence watches them leave holding his ball and booze.

EXT. TERRENCE APARTMENT/HALLWAY - LATER: Terrence stops at his door. He goes to unlock the door with his key. But no luck. It appears that the lock has been changed. HE TUGS ON HANDLE. HARDER. Still no luck. He signs. He moves back down the hallway, walks up to his manager's apartment door.

> ### TERRENCE (knocking on door)
> Mr. Smith! Mr. Smith! I think my key is broken.

Mr. Smith opens the door. Terrence stares at him.

> ### TERRENCE (cont'd)
> I can't get inside my apartment.

> ### MANAGER
> And why might that be?

> ### TERRENCE
> Well, I don't know, you tell me.

> ### MANAGER
> Okay, ummm I thought we had this conversation already.

> ### TERRENCE
> Unfortunately we didn't.

Terrence stares at him.

> ### MANAGER
> Terrence, I changed the lock myself.

> ### TERRENCE
> Oh, you did-did you?

> ### MANAGER
> I'm entitled, considering I'm the manager of the building and whenever a tenant –such as yourself,

fails to pay his rent on time, is unusually when I change the locks.

Terrence falls back.

> ### TERRENCE
> But I just paid you for the last two month and you said everything was fine.

> ### MANAGER
> You paid me for the previous two months and you're still behind for this month.

> ### TERRENCE
> I don't have anywhere to go.

Mr. Smith burst out laughing.

> ### TERRENCE (cont'd)
> I don't see what's so damn funny.

> ### MANAGER (sarcastically)
> Terrence, if you could see the look on your face you'd understand why I'm laughing.

> ### TERRENCE (mad)
> You're nothing but the damn devil.

> ### MANAGER
> You-can-go-right-a head and try to turn this whole situation around on me.

> ### TERRENCE
> Only the devil would laugh at a man who is down on his luck.

MANAGER

Terrence, this story about me being unfair to you, who gives a crap! Because as soon as we are done here, I'm going back in my room to get into my warm and comfortable bed.

Terrence is extremely irritated.

TERRENCE

Aaaaaa, you people kill me.

MANAGER

What do you mean by "you people?!"

TERRENCE

I have a very strong dislike towards you, haven't you noticed?

MANAGER

Careful.

TERRENCE (aggressive)

You're lucky I don't reach through this door and.....

MANAGER (pissed)

Okay-weirdo, so here is where I give you two seconds to get off my property.

TERRENCE

Oh-yeah? Who's gonna make me?!

He goes behind his door, pulls out a baseball bat.

MANAGER

One-one-thousand....

Terrence backs away and walks off...

                    MANAGER (devilish grin)
Have a nice life, Terrence.

He quickly moves down the hallway and exits.

EXT. TERRENCE'S SEDAN -CONTINUOUS: He stands at his car
dejected then gets inside, pulls off....

EXT. PLAYGROUND - CONTINUOUS: He pulls up next to playground,
shuts off car, gets out, moves to his trunk, OPENS TRUNK, PULLS OUT
A BLANKET. He returns to driver side, gets inside. He sits with blanket
halfway pulled up over him to keep him warm. He stares out at the courts.
There isn't a single sole insight. He GRABS HIS NBA BALL, gently rest his
head on the ball then slowly falls asleep.

INT. CANDACE HOUSE - CANDACE ROOM - CONTINUOUS:
Posters of USC ballers hanging up throughout her bedroom. A teddy bear
and a basketball lay on the pillow. Candace sits on ground between Jane's legs.
Jane fixes her hair before bed.

                        JANE
What's on your mind?

                      CANDACE
Nothing.

                        JANE
You seem awfully quiet.

                      CANDACE
I guess I'm just excited about our first game
tomorrow.

                        JANE
I knew there was something going on in that
brain of yours.

CANDACE

So since dad is coaching our new team, do I still have to call him dad?

Jane smiles.

CANDACE (cont'd)

You think the other players will make fun of me if I do call him dad?

JANE

Hum. That is a tough one.

CANDACE

I just want to make him proud.

JANE

Just do your best.

Candace sighs relief.

CANDACE

We met a guy at the playground today.

JANE

Really, was he any good?

CANDACE

Umm hum.

JANE

So, how'd you guys end up meeting?

CANDACE

I walked up to him and struck up a conversation while he was helping a injured teammate off the court.

JANE
Oh, so what did you guys talk about?

CANDACE
Mainly basketball.

JANE
Was your dad with you?

CANDACE
Umm humm.

JANE
Does this guy have a name?

CANDACE
Umm humm, his name is, Mr. Good.

JANE
Does he have a first name?

CANDACE
Terrence.

JANE
Terrence Good. Sounds good to me.

CANDACE
I really like him and he's a really good ball player.

JANE
Candace, if you don't mind me asking, what was the point of you telling me about this, Mr. Good.

CANDACE
I don't know, he just seems like a nice guy.

Jane sighs.

JANE

Candace, you already know how me and your father feel about you socializing with strangers.

CANDACE

I know mom...

Jane continues fixing Candace's hair.

INT. JANE'S BEDROOM - A SHORT TIME AFTER: Jane sits on her bed in her bedroom typing on her laptop. She does a Google search under Terrence's name. We she sees various sports articles about Terrence's high school basketball achievements. She sees a photo of him standing next to his high school teammates holding up a trophy that reads MVP. She is impressed.

INT. CANDACE HOUSE - KITCHEN - MORNING: Jane is cooking at the stove. Eggs, hash, and ham. Candace enters holding a gym bag and a basketball. Wears a "HANG TIME" jersey with the number "23".

JANE

Your breakfast is on the table.

CANDACE

Dads running late.

Candace moves to the counter, pulls open a drawer, grabs aluminum foil, walks up to the table, starts scraping eggs, hash, and ham off the plate with a fork and into the aluminum foil.

JANE

Not too much before the game, okay?

Candace nods. Jane stops at the table with pot and scoops out eggs, hash, and ham into the aluminum foil also.

JANE (cont'd)

...A little extra for your father.

Chad rushes by Candace, kisses Jane... looks at Candace. Wears a "HANG TIME" t-shirt and Cap. A whistle hangs around his neck.

CHAD (excited)

Are we ready to get a win today?

CANDACE

I was born ready.

CHAD

Faaaaantastic.

He does a funky little dance and chants: "HANG TIME"... "HANG TIME"... "HANG TIME"... Jane and Candace get in on the act, also excitedly chanting.... "HANG TIME".... "HANG TIME"..... He looks at Jane.

CHAD (cont'd)

Wish us luck, we're gonna need it.

Chad and Candace rush out the door...

INT. CHAD'S SUV -CONTINUOUS: Chad steers at the wheel...Candace sits, both munch on eggs, hash, and ham.

CANDACE (chewing)

Yummy in my tummy.

Candace stuffs a huge piece of hash in her mouth.

CHAD (cont'd)

Woooow!

She gives him a thumps up, continues MUNCHING.

INT. BASKETBALL GYM - CONTINUOUS: The bleachers are just about empty. Nine hang time team members warm up on the court — all standing five feet tall. Ten Asian American girl ballers, also standing five feet — the opposing team, are also warming up. Candace enters the gym first, then

Chad. Candace drops her bag next to her team's bench, then runs over to join her team mates in the warm up.

Chad gets all the girls in a big huddle.

CHAD

Okay girls, let's play smart and have some fun out there, play hard okay!

Hang time on three. One! Two! Three!

HANG TIME

Win!

All the players and coaches move to their bench for one final rally, then all the players move to center court. At center court, Candace glances at Chad. She slowly exhales then crouches down in a combative position as the ball is tossed up in the air.

INT. BASKETBALL GYM - CONTINUOUS: Fourth quarter. Three minutes to go... Hang time is getting beat by fifteen points. Candace dribbles in front of her opponent — she lacks confidence. The opponent steals the ball from her when she goes to pass it to a teammate, then lays it up. Chad makes angry gestures at Candace. Candace cowardly brings the ball up the court, again. She accidentally dribbles the ball off her sneaker. The opponent quickly picks up the ball and dribbles down the court to attempt a lay up, Candace tries desperately to block the opponent's shot. We hear a whistle!

REF

Blocking foul, number twenty-three. Two shots.

Chad yells-disagrees with the call. Candace sadly lowers her head. She takes a deep breath. She knells down, out of breath. Looks up at Chad.

CANDACE (cont'd)

I ran back on defense as fast as I could.

CHAD (stern)

It wasn't good enough.
And you still let them score.

Candace gives herself a pathetic pep rally, as she tries to gather her breath and regain her focus. She stands at the half court, as the opponent sinks both free throws.....Two second left in the game......The buzzer sounds. Hang time is defeated by a large margin. Chad glances at the scoreboard, he feels awful about the final outcome of the game.

INT. CANDACE'S HOUSE - CANDACE'S ROOM - NIGHT: Candace sits slumped on her bed in her PJ's. Jane enters.

JANE

Your father told me about what happened in your game.

CANDACE

I completely let him down.

She stares at her.

JANE

It was your first game with your dad, you'll have plenty of chances to prove yourself to him.

Candace stares at nothing.

JANE (tucks her in bed) (cont'd)

Hang in there okay...

INT. TERRENCE SEDAN -NIGHT: Terence sits, reading his NBA magazine.

Just then: A basketball HITS his driver side door. He quickly jumps up, a young boys runs up to his cars, picks up the ball.

YOUNG BOY

It was an accident.

He runs over to the courts. Terrence sees him. We see FIFTEEN MULTI-CULTURAL YOUNG BOYS playing a game on the courts. The young boys seem raw in their ability as they wildly tossing up the ball at the hoop. Terrence shakes his head, gets out of his car, heads over to them holding his NBA magazine. He stops at the sideline. A RADIO SITS NEXT TO THE SIDELINE PLAYING HEAVY METAL ROCK MUSIC. The boys start arguing at each other — total chaos, pushing and shoving one another. One boy rocks out with an imaginary guitar. Terrence whistles, they stop. He SHUTS OFF THE RADIO.

TERRENCE (shouts)

Okay, I want everyone to listen up! That means stop what you're doing until I've finished what I have to say! By a show of hands, who here would like to learn a thing or two about the game of basketball?

All the boys walk up to him and raise up their hands.

YOUNG BOY#1

Who the heck are you, Mr.?

TERRENCE

My name is Terence Good, and I too had dreams of playing in the NBA.

All the boys light up.

YOUNG BOY#1

Why did you stop playing ball?

YOUNG BOY#2

Yeah, what made you throw in the towel?

TERRENCE

It's complicated, however, I can reassure everyone that I have tons of knowledge and experience that can be of use to each and everyone of you — that's if you would like to use me as your guild.

All the boys, turn, and look at each other, Just then:

YOUNG BOY#1

We'd like to call a huddle first.

TERRENCE

Sure, take as much time as you need.

They huddle up to discuss... They break out....

YOUNG BOY#1

Okay, everyone said they're in favor of you being our coach.

TERRENCE

Wow! Really! Okay!

YOUNG BOY#1

So what happens now?

Terrence scratches his head.

TERRENCE

First, I'll need to evaluate each one of your capabilities — as a matter of fact, wait right here.

He runs to his car, pulls out his CLIPBOARD, moves back over to them.

TERRENCE (cont'd)

I need everyone to write down their last name and pick a number between one and fifteen.

He hands them his clipboard. They all take turns WRITING DOWN THEIR LAST NAME AND JERSEY NUMBER. They hand the clipboard back to Terrence. Terrence quickly looks at it, then looks up at them all.

TERRENCE (cont'd)

Now that I have everyone's information, lets meet back here on Saturday at 7AM to begin our first lesson.

YOUNG BOY#1

So, what will the name of our team be?

I'm so glad you asked and I have the perfect name:
Team Protégé.

They all approve. They all go back to playing ball on the court. Terrence confiscates the radio, then moves to his car and gets inside....

INT. TERRENCE SEDAN -MORNING: Terrence opens his eyes, looks at the courts, its empty. We hear his stomach GROWLING, looks down at his stomach.

TERRENCE

I guess that means it's feeding time.

He pulls out his wallets, opens it, he's flat broke. He gets out of his car, walks down the sidewalk, sits in front of a bank. He stares out... sees a women eating a candy bar...she tosses it in a nearby trash can...he looks around...then quickly runs up to the trash can, PICKS UP CANDY BAR — we see dirt particles covering the candy bar...he is ashamed..his stomach LOUDLY GROWLS like a safari lion. He looks around, sees a half-full beer bottle sitting on a bus stop... He SHOVES the candy bar in his month then rushes to the beer bottle, picks it up, CHUGS...

He pathetically moves down the sidewalks...see a preacher-man holding biblical tracks... walks up to him...

> PREACHER MAN (shouts)
> I'm a living witness that God is real!

> TERRENCE
> Can your God provide food and shelter for someone who really needs it?

The preacher man stares at him.

> TERRENCE (cont'd) (pathetic)
> I ask because I'm down and out.

> PREACHER MAN
> My God is a miracle worker.

Terrence leans in, serious. CHUGS beer...

> TERRENCE
> You wanna know something? I talk to God every-single-day, as a matter fact — we had a brief conversation this morning about how cruel and insensitive this world can be to someone who's just trying to get by. What would your God say to that huh?

> PREACHER MAN
> He will never leave or forsaken you.

He HANDS him a track, Terrence SLAPS IT OUT OF HIS HAND and angrily walks off...

INT. SPORT STORE — LATE AFTERNOON: Terrence stands in front of the counter, a MIDDLE AGE MAN stands behind the counter.

TERRENCE

Good afternoon, sir. I was looking around your
store and I came across these really cool basketball
jersey –sitting right over there.

He turns and points to a rack full of red basketball jerseys.

TERRENCE

You-see, I have this group, of about fifteen kids
and I was wondering if you would be interested
in donating the jerseys to them — sorta of like
giving back to the community.

MIDDLE AGE MAN

Seems like a nice gesture, and it just so happens
that my son plays basketball for his high school
team. But there's one thing I have to ask you.

TERRENCE

What's that?

MIDDLE AGE MAN

Would you happen to be referring to that rowdy
group of kids that play over at the park every
single day of the week?

Terrence nods.

MIDDLE AGE MAN (cont'd)

I thought so.

Terrence stares.

MIDDLE AGE MAN (cont'd)

I tell you what, I'll do it as a favor for you this
one time, so why don't you come back by here in
about an another hour, I'll have them sitting out
in a plastic bag next to the entrance.

Terrence is amazed.

TERRENCE
Ahh-man, you're not BS-ing me are, you?

MIDDLE AGE MAN
Anything for the children.

They shake.

TERRENCE
You're a good man.

Terrence exits.

EXT. SIDEWALK -MIDNIGHT: Terrence sits in-front of the bank, holding his NBA basketball, and writing on his clipboard. We see the plastic bag full of jerseys sitting next to him.

TERRENCE
Now according to Antonio, team Protégé talents and capabilities should go something like this:

CLIPBOARD CLOSE:

(1) LEO (PROTÉGÉ): TIMING
(2) DAVIS (PROTÉGÉ): MENTAL TOUGHNESS
(3) CLARK (PROTÉGÉ): HAND SPEED
(4) BOLTON (PROTÉGÉ): DEFENSE
(5) SEALY (PROTÉGÉ): GRIT
(6) MILLER (PROTÉGÉ): REBOUNDING
(7) BRAND (PROTÉGÉ): COORDINATION
(8) HOWARD (PROTÉGÉ): SPEED
(9) BLAKELY (PROTÉGÉ): QUICKNESS
(10) CRAIG (PROTÉGÉ): MENTAL TOUGHNESS
(11) WILSON (PROTÉGÉ): HANDS
(12) MITCHELL (PROTÉGÉ): FEET
(13) ANDERSON (PROTÉGÉ): SPEED

(14) JOHNSON (PROTÉGÉ): REBOUNDING
(15) THOMPSON (PROTÉGÉ): COURAGE.

...It starts raining. Terrence looks for shelter...gets up and sits by an alleyway. He continues writing... He has several flashbacks of different basketball lessons with Harrison when he was a kid... He becomes emotional as he continues writing. He hears a ripple of extremely loud gunshots in the ally. Terrence is frighten, he jumps up and runs away, stops in-front of an apartment building. DRENCHING WET, HE NERVOUSLY CLUTCHES HIS BALLAND CLIPBOARD... STARTS CRYING FRANTICALLY...

TERRENCE (shivering)
Dad, where are you, I'm so scared..

He hear gunshots again... Terrence sees a robbery taking place right before his very own eyes... He cries harder and clutches his basketball tighter...

TERRENCE
I really need you right now.

He crouches down and falls to the ground, still shivering...

"SATURDAY" then "7AM"

EXT. PLAYGROUND -CONTINUOUS: Terrence is out cold on the court holding his basketball and clipboard... a bottle of booze sits next to him. He rest his head on the plastic bag full of jerseys. Team Protégé:All fifteen boys walk up to him.

YOUNG BOY #1
Hey look, we got ourselves a town drunk.

All the boys laugh at him. Terrence opens his eyes..

TERRENCE

Hey I heard that, I'm alert-I'm alert. I have all your capabilities written down on my clipboard as promised.

YOUNG BOY #1

You keep it. Town drunk....! Town drunk....! Town drunk....!

He turns to his crew...

YOUNG BOY#1 (cont'd)

Let's blow this joint.

One of the boys smoke pot. They all walk off. Another boy runs up to him and kicks him in his butt then snatches the bag of jerseys up and pulls out a jersey.

YOUNG BOY#2

Cool, he got us new jerseys.

All the boys walk off as they each reach down in the bag and pull out the jerseys and share them amongst each other. Candace is on the court training with Chad. Chad passes her the ball, it slips through Candace's hands...she goes chasing after it...

The basketball rolls up to a AFRICAN AMERICAN FEMALE, GABBY. She picks up the ball, Candace walks up to her.

GABBY (stern)

Do you wanna be here, kid?

Candace looks up at her.

GABBY (cont'd)

I've been standing over here watching you for the past hour and It just doesn't seem like you're putting fort much effort.

Candace is unsure.

> #### GABBY (cont'd)
> Effort is the use of physical or mental energy to do something. Better known as, will.

Gabby leans in.

> #### GABBY (cont'd) (whispers to Candace)
> Is your mommy and daddy putting you up to this?

Candace quickly backs away, she shakes her head.

> #### GABBY (cont'd)
> C'mon you don't have to play shy with me, tell me the truth. I bet you'd rather be at home putting together a crossword puzzle.

> #### CANDACE (shakes her head)
> When I was born the doctor told my dad that I had the heart of a million lions.

> #### GABBY
> Oh really? Is-that-so?A million lions huh?

Candace quickly nods.

> #### GABBY
> So then how about you take every single one of those millions of lions. (points at Candace's chest) And try to make just one shot.

She hands Candace the basketball, Candace slowly looks up at the hoop — she feels it's a milestone.

> #### CANDACE (discouraged)
> I can't because coach Mayday told me that I was too short to play for him.

GABBY

If you try, you can.

Chad walks up to them.

CHAD (stern) (to Candace)

How many time... just how many times do I have to tell you not to talk to strangers, Candace?

Gabby looks at Chad.

GABBY

I'm sorry, and you are?

CHAD

I happen to be this little girl's father.

GABBY

We were just having a small chat.

Candace sulks, and then Gabby reconsiders.

GABBY (cont'd)

"Small" probably wasn't a good choice of words.

CHAD

The last coach I had her with wrecked her confidence, so now I have to try to reverse the effects and boy is it not easy. But, I bet someone like yourself never had a coach flat out tell you- you weren't good enough.

She pulls out her cell phone, does a quick Google search of her profile. She hands him her cell phone

GABBY

I think you have your facts about me misconstrued, please read my profile.

Chad is shocked as he reads her rags to riches story. He hands the phone back to her.

                              CHAD
          I owe you an apology.

He knells down in front of her. She quickly pulls him up.

                              GABBY
          I'm flattered.

                              CHAD
          You're like an angel sent from heaven.

                              GABBY
          So they say.

                              CHAD
          Must have been a pretty hard road, now look
          at you.

                              GABBY
          If I can do it, she can do it.

She knells down in front of Candace. She walks off...

                              CHAD
          So, umm, I'm gonna head back over to the court.

He walks off. Candace sees Terrence laying on the ground. She heads over to him. She walks up to Terrence.

                              CANDACE
          Mr. Good, why are you laying on the ground?

Terrence slowly looks a up at her, then glances at Chad in the distance.

                    TERRENCE

Oh, hey Candace ... I didn't know you had practice
with your dad today.

                    CANDACE

We pretty much practice here every Saturday.

Candace reaches out her hand to help him up. He is embarrassed.

        TERRENCE (cont'd)(fights tears)

I think I'm gonna just sit here for a second and
think about my life — where it's headed etc...

                    CANDACE

Suite yourself.

                    TERRENCE

If your father ask, you didn't see me okay.

                    CANDACE

Okay.

Coach Mayday appears on the court next to them with eight ten year boys
as they run lines up and down the court. Candace notices them...nervously
stares...

                CANDACE (cont'd)

Oh boy, there goes my old coach.

Terrence looks at him. He raises up and stands next to Candace.

                    TERRENCE

He knows his stuff.

                    CANDACE

Him and my dad don't get along anymore.

They both watch as coach Mayday runs intense drills after drills in his practice.

                        TERRENCE
Your pops seem like a nice guy, why wouldn't they
get along?

                        CANDACE
He cut me from his team.

                        TERRENCE
Any particular reason, why?

                        CANDACE
He told my dad that I wasn't tall enough to play
for him anymore.

                        TERRENCE
That must of hurt.

Chad gestures Candace over to him.

                        CANDACE
Well, I gotta get back to my workout.

                        TERRENCE
You tell your dad that I'll be in touch.

She walks off... Terrence FROWNS at coach Mayday.... She returns...

                        CANDACE
I almost forgot to give you this.

SHE HANDS HIM A HANDMADE FRIENDSHIP BRACELET. He
CLASP THE BRACKET.

                        TERRENCE
Thanks for the gift.

She walks off again. He reaches down and picks up his clipboard, he scribbles
on the clipboard the words: (16) FUKUMI (PROTÉGÉ):?

In a desperate attempt to reveal Candace's special talent and special gift, he comes up with nothing at the moment.

EXT. SIDEWALK - LATER: Terrence sits in front of the bank, listening to RAP music on his radio. He sees TWO HOMELESS MEN ARGUING ACROSS THE STREET IN FULL COLOR. HE TURNS UP THE VOLUME ON THE RADIO. The two men throw punches at each other. Terrence gets in on the act — throws air punches in the direction of both men.

> TERRENCE
> I got my money on the bald guy.

A AFRICAN AMERICAN MAN DROPS A BUCKET NEXT TO TERRENCE AND THEN HOLDS A SIGN THAT READS "I WILL SING FOR FOOD".

> AFRICAN AMERICAN MAN
> You don't mind if I pan-handle here do you? I was told by the locals that this spot was pretty low key.

Terrence changes stations.

> TERRENCE
> It's a free country.

> AFRICAN AMERICAN MAN
> Very kind of you, sir.

He begins warming up his pipes. Looks at Terrence.

> AFRICAN AMERICAN MAN (cont'd)
> Do you have a special song request?

> TERRENCE
> You got any love songs?

> AFRICAN AMERICAN MAN
> Let me see what I can whip up.

Terrence continues changing stations... the man starts singing a spiritually-soft John Legend tune. Terrence slowly looks up at him. Amazed.

TERRENCE (snapping his finger)
Music to my ears-music to my ears.

The man goes all out, singing with his heart and soul. A bunch of dollar bills tossed into his bucket by people passing by. Terrence gets up, grabs his basketball and smoothly slow dances with his basketball... gliding and swaying back and forth to the man's rich voice. He is oblivious as he reminisces about his high school flame Tina. He sits down, and continues to sway to the spiritual tune. John Legend walks by with his wife, DROPS a one hundred dollar bill in front of Terrence.

JOHN LEGEND
Cool sounds, man.

A couple of hipsters move pass him. He see the one hundred dollar bill, picks it up, runs after John Legend.

TERRENCE (shouts)
Mr. Legend! Wait! This money doesn't belong to me. I'm not the one singing the song.

He stops, fatigued. Looks around, spots a HOMELESS INDIAN WOMEN with THREE YOUNG GIRLS near a hot dog stand. His stomach GROWLS... He winces in pain. HE GLANCES AT HIS FRIENDSHIP BRACELET, then moves toward them. He stands behind a MAN AND A WOMEN waiting to order. He walks up to the counter as the man and women walk away. He studies the menu. He orders a hotdog and a coke. The grand total of the hotdog and coke is: $4.00. The cashier gives him his change. He looks at the homeless women.

Then:

TERRENCE (cont'd)
Miss, I don't mean you any harm, but, I want you to have it.

He hands her the all the change in his hand.

> ### MIDDLE AGE WOMAN
> Thank you, thank you very much.

> ### TERRENCE
> Anytime.

She glances at her daughters.

> ### MIDDLE AGE WOMAN
> They keep me young.

> ### TERRENCE
> They're beautiful, you take care of yourself.

Terrence watches them as they move toward the hot dog stand. He half-smiles.

He knells down on his knees, closes his eyes and begins PRAYING OVER HIS FOOD. He opens his eyes and takes a bite of the hotdog.

Then:

He turns and sees Tina moving down the sidewalk with TWO OF HER MODEL FRIENDS as they head to a nightclub. She is dressed to kill. She is, radiant. He looks up at the sky.

> ### TERRENCE
> How did you know?

He walks up to her from behind, TAPS her on her shoulder. She turns to face him.

> ### TINA (shocked)
> Oh-my-God, it's really you, what part of stop stalking me on my Facebook did you not understand?

Terrence is confused.

TERRENCE
Facebook? Tina, its me, Terrence.
Your old high school boyfriend.
We had a falling out just before you left to Yale?

Her mouth drops wide open.

TINA
...Terrence, oh-my-wow, I thought you were this
jerk whose been stalking me on Facebook, — I
didn't even recognize you.

She covers her nose in disgust.

TINA (cont'd)
No offense but you smell and look terrible.
Carl had told me you up and moved out of state
for some semi-pro basketball tryout.

TERRENCE

That's not true, I've been here in Los Angeles all this time.

TINA (still covering her nose)

This is so weird, the one night I decide to celebrate my first successful art exhibition I end up running into my X.

TERRENCE

You sold your first art piece? Congratulations! When we were in high school you use to always talk about how bad you wanted to have your own art gallery someday, — I'm so happy for you..

Her friends become antsy. They look Terrence up and down.

FRIEND #1(covering her nose)

Tina, were gonna be late for the show.

Tina glances at Terrence's radio and clipboard sitting next to the African man in the distance. She stares at him, serious.

TINA (disbelief) (still covering her nose)

Are you living out here on the street?

TERRENCE

It's complicated.

TINA

When is the last time you had a bath and a hot meal?

TERRENCE

I'm actually in the middle of my dinner as we speak.

He holds up his half-bitten hotdog. She back away even more disgusted — still covering her nose.

> ### TINA
> That's disgusting.

He stares at her.

> ### TINA (cont'd)
> If you need a place to stay you can crash at my apartment until you get back on your feet.

> ### TERRENCE (cont'd)
> You don't have to worry about me, okay.

> ### FRIEND #1
> Tina, hello?!

Tina glances at her.

> ### TINA
> Give us a second.

She looks at Terrence, reaches in her purse, pulls out her business card.

> ### TINA (cont'd)
> We gotta get going, here's my card, call me — it'll be good to catch up on old times.

She hands it to him.

> ### TERRENCE
> Congratulations once again.

They walk off. He exhales.

EXT. SIDEWALK -CONTINUOUS: Terrence sits, staring at Tina's business card as the African man gathers his belongs.

AFRICAN AMERICAN MAN

I don't mean to pry, but was that nice looking young girl you were talking to earlier your girlfriend? Man, she's absolutely beautiful.

TERRENCE

We were an item in high school and then I did something very stupid and she ended up leaving me and moving on with her life.

AFRICAN AMERICAN MAN

Well, it must not have been that bad, she gave you her card to call her.

TERRENCE

I guess you're right, it must not have been that bad.

AFRICAN AMERICAN MAN

Whenever all hell breaks loose you have two ways you can look at it. The first would be that everything happens for a reason and the second would be that everything happens for a reason.

TERRENCE

I see your point.

AFRICAN AMERICAN MAN

Let me put it to you this way, very few men get a second chance with the women of their dreams.

Terrence stares at the card.

AFRICAN AMERICAN MAN (cont'd)

That's my time, thanks for letting me tag alone.

He hands Terrence a twenty dollar bill.

                         TERRENCE
Where you headed?

                    AFRICAN AMERICAN MAN
I'll be around.

He walks off. Terrence moves over to a payphone. He dials Tina's number...
she picks up...

                       TINA (in phone)
Wow, that was fast, so I guess you really care
about me after all.

                     TERRENCE (in phone)
Would you like some company?

                          TINA
Yeah-okay.

INT. TINA'S APARTMENT-KITCHEN - CONTINUOUS: Tina stands
at the stove cooking steak and mash potatoes. Soft music plays underneath.

INT. TINA'S APARTMENT-BATHROOM - CONTINUOUS: Terrence
lathers himself up with hand soap and sings in the shower.

INT. TINA'S APARTMENT-KITCHEN - CONTINUOUS: Tina
prepares a candle lite dinner, she sets the table with a silk table mat and
utensils. She sets down a bottle of red wine and two wine glasses. Everything
looks really nice. Terrence enters the kitchen wearing his old high school team's
practice jersey and gym shorts. Tina looks at him and half-smiles.

                          TINA
Can't believe they still fit you.

                    TERRENCE (half-smiling)
....And I can't believe you held on to them after
all these years.

TINA

Lets just say that they bring back good memories.

He looks down at the table setting.

TERRENCE

What do we have here? Ummm-umm-ummm. I
am starving, everything looks and smells delicious.

He rushes to table, sits down, she sits down as well. She tucks a napkin in his
shirt collar. He GRABS at a biscuit.

She SMACKS HIS HAND.

TINA

Not before we say grace.

They bow their heads and say grace together.

She looks up at him, and giggles.

Then:

TINA (cont'd)

Bonbon appetite.

TERRENCE

Bonbon appetite.

He grabs a biscuit and eats it with his steak and potato. She just sits back and
smiles at him. She sips red wine.

TINA

After the show tonight me and my girls went
to this club that got rave reviews on Yelp. The
minute we walked in, there was this gentleman
who took our coats and showed us to the bar and
that's where things got a little crazy. This guy

came up to me and asked me if he could buy me a drink and he started kissing on my hand and getting a little too personal.

If you know what I mean. Oh, I was so ready to leave after that happened, you have no idea. So one of my girlfriends butted in between us and told him that she was my date for the night — it worked like a charm. He ended up jetting off and we didn't see him for the rest of the night. There are times I find myself thinking about what we had, and what I missed about us the most is that regardless of my mood swings you were always the perfect gentleman to me, and I thank you for that.

She gently rubs his face. He half-smiles.

TINA (cont'd)
So, how's your family and friends?

TERRENCE
It's been several years since I heard back from my pops. As for my friends, De-rock moved to Atlanta and Carl was passed down a large sum of money from his grandfather who passed away about three years ago –talk about living it up in the Hamptons. Man, why can't I have that kind of luck.

TINA
The grass isn't always greener on the other side.

Terrence absorbs this.

TERRENCE
Yeah but having that kind of money can make things a whole lot easier in my day-to-day grind.

He looks around her apartment. He looks at her.

TINA

It must be pretty hard living on the street.

TERRENCE

Some days are a little easier than others.

TINA

How long has it been?

TERRENCE

Nine months.

TINA (sighs)

The important thing is that you're alive.

TERRENCE

Amen.

TERRENCE (cont'd)

I'd like to make a toast to our reunion and much success to you and your art career.

TINA (jokily)

Who said anything about this being a reunion?

TERRENCE (laughing)

I just did.

They laugh. They toast. They sip red wine.

TERRENCE (cont'd)

How would you feel if I told you that I've been offered a coaching job?

TINA (half-smiling)

I think you would make a great mentor.

TERRENCE (nodding)

That means alot to me.

TINA

Is that it?

TERRENCE

Pretty much. Yep.

He glances at the clock hanging on the wall. He feels he has overstayed his welcome.

TERRENCE (cont'd)

I think I should be heading out.

He raises up. She GENTLY GRABS HIS HAND, pulls him back down.

TINA

Stay the night.

He slides back down in his chair, they both sip red wine.

EXT. BASKETBALL GYM -DAY: Candace dribbles the ball with ten seconds left in the game. Hang Time down 2. Chad calls a timeout. All the players move to their bench. In Hang Time's huddle:

CHAD

Candace, I want you to inbound the ball to Becky. The minute she catches it, you step in bounds and spot up for the three.

Candace nods. They break out. Candace stands out of bounds, Candace's team mates stand at center court in a single-file-line. Candace slaps the ball hard, the players scrabble to different areas on the court. Candace sees Becky, she inbounds the ball to her then steps in bounds near the three point line. Becky passes her the ball back. Candace catches the ball. glances at the shot clock, 3 seconds left...she looks at the hoop. She thinks it's no way possible she can make the shot.

CANDACE

Coach Mayday was right, I'll never be any good
at this game.

She unconsciously heaves the ball at the hoop, it air balls. The buzzer rings!
Chad gets extremely upset, he walks onto the court and stops in front of her.
He looks her dead in the eye.

CHAD (furious)

What just happened?!!! Unbelievable!!!

He walks off the court, extremely pissed.

"ONE MONTH LATER"

EXT. BASKETBALL COURT -MORNING: Terrence stands holding his
clipboard and NBA basketball. Tina walks away, gestures: "good bye". He
waves back at her, then looks straight ahead.

TERRENCE (shouts)

Okay, listen up! That means stop what you're
doing until I've finished what I have to say!

He looks down at his clipboard, then looks up.

TERRENCE (cont'd)

By a show of hands, who here would like to learn
a thing or two about the game of basketball?

Candace stands in front of him, she raises her hand.

CANDACE (soft)

Mr. Good, you don't have to yell because I'm
standing right in front of you.

He half-smiles.

TERRENCE

Oh, sorry.

CANDACE

Let's get this show on the road.

CHAPTER THREE

"CANDACE SENIOR YEAR"

INT. MEDD HIGH BASKETBALL GYM - MORNING: Championship flags hang down from the ceiling. Candace sits on the bleachers. She is 17 years old. Terrence sit on ground in front of her, next to his radio. He is 28 years old. He is cool-calm-relaxed. Candace begins stretching out her arms.

Terrence CLICKS ON the radio, we hear a classical tune.

> ### TERRENCE
> Look, there's something you need to know about me. I am an avid fan of classical music. And unless you want to see my mean side in today's training I suggest you work your tale off.

She looks serious.

> ### TERRENCE (cont'd)
> Over the years I've learned that when it comes to certain types of music and the game of basketball greatness can be achieved.

Candace just stares at him, extremely cocky. Extremely ready to take on whatever Terrence throws at her.

> ### TERRENCE (cont'd)
> I made your father a very special promise when you were ten years old — that I would see to it

that you gave me every bit of your heart, soul, love for the game for basketball and deliver for your teammates in crunch time.

TERRENCE (cont'd)
The same way I lead my highschool team to the state finals back 2012 — before I decided to quit the team a year later. My decision to quit should have nothing to do with your ability to lead your team to the CIF championship this season.

CANDACE NODS.

TERRENCE (cont'd)
Hopefully you don't hate me too bad when your mom and dad are sitting in the stance next year—cheering you on and I'll probably be at some sports bar watching you on the television while tilting back a cold one.

Candace stares at him.

TERRENCE
You might get a little homesick.

Candace grabs her basketball, squeezes it hard. Grits her teeth. Ready to rock.

TERRENCE
Hard work pays off.

Candace nods, accepting the challenge.

EXT. TRACK - EARLY MORNING: Candace runs fast along the track. Terrence stands near the track:

TERRENCE (cont'd)
Move your tale! Faster! Faster!

Candace moves faster....grimacing, but keeping up a rapid pace...

TERRENCE (cont'd)

Show me you want it! Because I don't think you do.

INT. BASKETBALL GYM - MORNING: Ball handling drills. Terrence yells.

TERRENCE

Hard work! Hard work! Hard work!

Candace does fancy-tricks in a ball handling drill in between rectangular shaped orange cones...

TERRENCE (cont'd)

That's it, you got it!

Candace dribbles the ball in between cones full speed ahead.

TERRENCE (cont'd)

You're gonna be an all star, kid!

She puts the ball down on the ground, then slams down to the ground, does 20 push ups...

CANDACE (loudly) (cont'd)
Aaaaaaaaaaa!

INT. WEIGHT ROOM - LATE DAY: Candace is lifting weights. She easily pushes up thirty pounds. Terrence stands behind her assisting.

TERRENCE
Breathe, easy now-easy...

She sets the weight in Terrence's hand.

TERRENCE (cont'd)
Good job!

CANDACE
My coach has been on my case in practice about finishing first in every drill.

TERRENCE

It's your coaches job to stay on top of things.

Candace exhales, fatigued.

CANDACE

Will he ever cut me some slack?

TERRENCE

Yeah, when you're dead. No, I'm kidding. Your coach wants to see you succeed, so don't take it personal, alright?

CANDACE

That's my problem, I take everything personal...

TERRENCE

Let's get back to work.

Candace lays back down underneath the thirty pound weight bar. She grips the weight bar, and lifts the weights off the rack again as Terrence spots her.

EXT. MEDD CAMPUS - LATE MORNING: Terrence walks Candace to her class.

CANDACE

So when is the big date for the wedding?

TERRENCE

We're still deciding.

CANDACE

Have you decided on how many people you plan on inviting?

TERRENCE (jokily)

Tina made it very clear that she would be handling all the invitations to our friends and family, I just going along for the ride I guess.

CANDACE

I'm available If she needs any help with all the fixings.

Terrence smiles.

TERRENCE

I will definitely let her know you offered your services.

CANDACE

It must be nice to have found that special someone, how long has it been anyway?

TERRENCE

Today marks our tenth anniversary together.

CANDACE

Really, has it been that long?

TERRENCE

Yep! You know what they say, time flies when you're in love.

CANDACE

I thought the saying was time flies when you're having fun.

TERRENCE

Yeah, that too.

CANDACE

Oh, before I forget, my dad is having a little get
together in a couple of weeks and it would be
nice if you and Tina can come by and maybe say
hello, I know mom and dad would be delighted
to finally meet her.

Terrence half-smiles.

TERRENCE

I'll be sure to let her know.

CANDACE

There's gonna be tons of cool people there.
Including a full band and open bar.

He cuts his eyes at her.

TERRENCE

Even if you were old enough I still wouldn't let
you have alcohol.

CANDACE (makes gestures)

Not even a tiny-little sip?

TERRENCE (stern)

Absolutely not.

She sighs and walks into her classroom.

INT. MEDD BASKETBALL GYM - MORNING: A intense scrimmage
between the starting line up and the bench players. CANDACE is playing the
point position with the starters. She battles at the guard against her backup,
JASMINE — AFRICAN AMERICAN, athletically built. Jasmine hounds
Candace as she dribbles the ball up the court, reaching at the ball, pushing
and shoving her around as she tries to keep her in front of her. Candace does a
tenacious spin move and rocks Sam on her heels. She pulls up for a mid-range
jumper. Swish!

COACH JONES

Sweet move, Candace!

Jasmine sulks as she sprints down the court. She tries to cut to the middle of the lane, but Candace cracks her hard in the rib with her forearm, knocking her slightly off balance. Jessica catches the ball, Candace rips it out of her hands and drives in it for a reverse lay up.

COACH JONES (cont'd)

Jasmine! Do I need to have you switch mans?

Jasmine, knells down grabbing her ribs in discomfort.

JASMINE (cont'd)

It won't happen again coach.

Jasmine walks up to Candace — gets up in her face.

JASMINE (cont'd)

You think you tough? Just remember where you come from, little miss China Town.

CANDACE (pissed)

Just shut up and play ball.

JASMINE

Ooooo now you talking mama.

She cheap shots Candace in the stomach.

Candace gets upset, walks up to her

CANDACE (cont'd) (pissed)

Hey, you got a problem with me? Where suppose to be teammate.

COACH JONES

Hey! Hey! That's enough you two, we play as a team, where in this together...

JASMINE (smacks candace's buns)

My bad, just wanted to see if I could get inside your head, obviously I won that battle.

She snickers at her.

CANDACE

Yeah, whatever.

Candace walks off, pissed....Coach Jones blows his whistle and the scrimmage continues...

INT. LOCKER ROOM - LATER: Candace gets dressed on the bench in front of her locker. Jasmine sits next to her.

JASMINE

We cool right?

CANDACE

Yeah, we cool.

JASMINE

You know I gotta give you a hard time while coach is riding my butt.

They laugh. Jasmine puts her arm around her.

CANDACE

I guess that's what I get for trying too hard. I hope you didn't take anything that I said personal.

JASMINE

Now why would I take "you busting me in my chops personal?"

CANDACE

Sorry, sometimes I forget were just scrimmaging and not in the actual game.

JASMINE

Don't worry about it.

Candace holds her hand up high, Jasmine clasp her hand.

CANDACE

Like coach said we're in this together.

Jasmine gets up and walks off.

INT. TINA'S APARTMENT - LIVINGROOM - NIGHT: Tina is (26) and Terrence sit bug eyed, cuddled up on her sofa intently watching a horror flick. Tina hold a bucket of popcorn. Terrence holds a soda pop and sips from two straws, Tina leans over and share his straw and sip.

TERRENCE

The first person to die in this movie is going to be the brotha.

TINA

I definitely disagree with you, my bet is on the tall blond chick.

TERRENCE

Double or nothing?

TINA

Double or nothing.

TERRENCE

Then again you can never tell with these B movies.

Terrence cell phone BEEPS as he receives a incoming text from Candace. CELL PHONE CLOSE: "Are you guys coming to the party?".

> ## TINA
> Who is that texting you,? I thought we agreed on no cell phone usage during movie night.

> ## TERRENCE (checking his messages)
> That we did, however this one is for you.

He hands cell phone to her. She reads Candace's message.

> ## TERRENCE (cont'd)
> Candace invited us to a get together with her folks. I told her I would check with you first and that we would only be able to attend if you said okay.

> ## TINA (squeezes his cheek)
> Oooo I trained you well, you are such a good boy.

As they continue watching the tube... they notice the African American male screaming to his death.

> ## TERRENCE
> Umm-Umm, see I told you, they just killed off the brotha.

She looks at him and hands his cell phone back to him, looks at tube.

> ## TINA (cont'd)
> Are you serious? Was it the tall blond chick who axed him off?

> ## TERRENCE
> Nope, it was his mother in law. So are we going to the party or what?

She stares at the tube, then quickly jumps up extremely frightened. Popcorn spills all over Terrence and he burst out laughing at her.

TINA (laughing)

Aw man, I must have seen this moving over a thousand times and that part always seem to send chills down my spine.

He makes chicken noises and flaps both his arm intimating a chicken.

TERRENCE

I'll save you.

He wraps her up in his arms.

TERRENCE (cont'd)

Come to daddy.

TINA enjoys his touch.

TINA (nodding)

I think we should go, you just never know who might show up.

Terrence kisses her on her neck.

TERRENCE

I don't think it's that kind of party, as a matter of fact I'm certain it's not, I've known the Fukumi family for quite some time now, were talking about my second family here.

She rubs his neck.

TINA

I'd be delighted to meet your second family and I think the timing couldn't be better with us getting married in a couple of months.

TERRENCE

Candace is sort of like a little sister to me. I really value the relationship that I have with her and her family, that young lady has taught me so much about life I feel like I owe her everything.

She feeds him popcorn. He gives her a sip of soda pop. They are the perfect couple.

TINA

Then I definitely can't wait to meet her too.

TERRENCE (kisses her cheek)

And so you shall.

TINA (cont'd)

I'm thinking about planning a trip for us to Hawaii as a pre honey-moon get away for the soon to be Mr. and Mrs. Good.

Terrence looks surprised, rubs her on her shoulders.

She rubs his hand. They cuddle up and go back to watching the tube.

INT. MEDD HIGH BASKETBALL COURT: A raucous crowd. Medd vs. Hamilton. Candace pulls up for a jumper, bottom of the net! She steals the inbound, drives to hoop for a uncontested lay up. She sprints back on defense...

EXT. SUBURBAN NEIGHBORHOOD – CONTINUOUS: Candace and Jasmine move down the sidewalk carrying backpacks.

Jasmine Abruptly,

JASMINE

Man, you killed Hamilton's team tonight. I bet you recorded a triple double. In between the legs reverse lay up and hitting from the outside, sweet!

CANDACE

Thanks, just doing my part.

JASMINE

So, what's going on with the fall dance? You have a date yet? I heard-it-to–the-grapevine that Arthur Chandler asked Susie Harrison to the dance.

CANDACE

Who's, Arthur Chandler?

JASMINE (excited)

Okay, news flash! Arthur Chandler is like the coolest-cutest-hottest hunk of a man-child to ever attend mercy high school and plus he has the most adorable eyes.

CANDACE

If that's what you're going for.

JASMINE (changes the topic)

While in other news — I overheard the most outlandish conversation between Mr. Celtic and Mrs. Lee in regards to the number of foreign exchange students they secretly invite over to their house during after school hours — due to some extended research project. I later learned that this has been going on for about two years— and to make matters even more gossipy — were you aware that our Principal Mr. Jacob has been dating a seventeen year old foreign exchange student from Honduras?

Candace shakes her head.

JASMINE (cont'd)

So I decided to ask my mom what she thought about our teachers and different staff members leading double lives, and you wanna know what her response was?

CANDACE

Sure why not.

JASMINE (beat)

It was the most ridiculous riddle I think I ever heard in my entire life.

Candace considers this. They stop. CANDACE STARES AT JASMINE.

CANDACE

I'm curious to hear more about this ridiculous riddle.

JASMINE

Okay, so it went something like this — if Mr. Celtic's shame was bright orange and Mrs. Lee's shame was green and Mr. Jacob's shame was red, and finally — the Honduran foreign exchange student's shame was yellow. Then who do you side with?

CANDACE

That's simple, neither one...

JASMINE IS UNSURE. She puts on RED lipstick. CANDACE STARES AT JASMINE'S FACE AS SHE PUTS ON HER LIP STICK.

Candace sees Jasmine's face as a silhouette.

CANDACE (cont'd)

It all depends on how you interpret the word color.

Jasmine is completely confused. They continue walking...

INT. CANDACE'S ROOM - NIGHT: Candace is on the bed, studying "BLACK HISTORY".

Through Candace's point-of view. The pages of the book are silhouette. Jane enters the bedroom. She wears evening attire.

> ### JANE
> Candace, your dad and I are heading over to the Wilson's for dinner tonight. Melissa will be staying at a friend's sleepover.

Candace just stares into her text book.

> ### JANE (cont'd)
> Candace, did you hear me?

Candace nods. JANE exits the room. Candace shuts the text book, she is fatigued. She gets up and turns on the television –- flips channels. She stop on a news broadcasting discussing "race relations".

Candace looks at the tube and figures in the tube are silhouette in color.

INT. NIGHTCLUB - CONTINUOUS: POP MUSIC on a jukebox. Terrence stands at the bar next to Tina — they both sip martinis.

> ### TINA (Half-Drunken)
> So how about we have a little nightcap at my place tiger? Raaaaa!

Terrence is blushing.

She FONDLES his ear, he pulls back, glances at his CELL PHONE — sitting on the bar.

> ### TINA (cont'd)
> I am so lucky to have you in my life.

She PULLS him in close. She kiss him.

His CELL PHONE FLASHES AN INCOMING CALL. The caller ID reads — FUKUMI. He picks up his phone, BEEPS ON.

                    TERRENCE (cont'd)
Candace, what a pleasant surprise, what's new?

                    CANDACE (into phone)
Oh, nothing much. Just sitting here watching the tonight show. Is this a good time? I hear a lot of noise in the background.

Tina is whispering something naughty in his ear.

                    CANDACE
Maybe I should call you back.

Tina blows in his ear, Terrence giggles.

                    TERRENCE (panting)
Tina and I are out having drinks.

                    TINA
I'm gonna go tinkle, be right back.

She walks off...

                    CANDACE
There's something I wanna ask you.

                    TERRENCE
Shoot!

                    CANDACE
Jasmine invited me out to a house party tomorrow night. I'm not sure if I should go.

                    TERRENCE (into phone)
Oh, well, have you talked it over with your folks???

CANDACE (into phone)
Umm, not yet.

He considers this...

TERRENCE (into phone)
I think you'd be better off discussing something like this with your mom and dad.

CANDACE (into phone)
Okay, just thought I'd ask.

TERRENCE (into phone)
I'll talk to you later.

He beeps off. Tina walks up to him. Stunning!

TINA
Now, where were we?

They kiss.

INT. COUNSELORS OFFICE - AFTERNOON: Candace sits across from her counselor –- who is looking over Candace's progress report. Candace stares at her.

CANDACE
Is there any reason why this couldn't wait until after my basketball practice?

COUNSELOR (half-smiles)
Yes there is...

Candace slowly emerges from her counselor's officer — staring down at a letter. Jasmine runs by.

JASMINE (loudly)
I'll pick you up at eight tonight!

CANDACE
Great news! I made the dean's list!

Jasmine runs down the hall.

"HOUSE PARTY"

INT. HOUSE PARTY, DEN - NIGHT: LOUD retro funk music.

Candace slouches on a leather couch, wears a low cut blouse and jeans. She is watching ESPN on the tube. Figures in the television as a silhouette. Jasmine enters the room, disappointingly looks at her.

JASMINE
I can't believe you're actually sitting here watching this crap while the party of the century is right outside these four walls. Candace, how do you expect for any of the guys here to-get-to-know-you if you're just gonna be antisocial?

Candace just stares at the tube. This is when a TALL SLENDER AFRICAN AMERICAN TEENAGER enters the room – passing by Jasmine — heading straight for Candace. He throws Jasmine a devilish smirk. Candace is completely absorbed into the tube. He sits next to Candace. Jasmine is speechless.

ARTHUR CHANDLER
So, I hear you put up big numbers the other night against our conference rivals –- pretty impressive for a girl.

Jasmine gestures to Candace: "That's him!" Candace continues watching the tube. Arthur Chandler feels neglected.

ARTHUR CHANDLER (cont'd)
You don't have to play shy with me sunshine. I promise I'll be gentle, scouts honor.

He LOOKS down Candace's blouse. He goes in for the kiss. Candace SMACKS him across the face. Hard. He jumps up, upset.

ARTHUR CHANDLER (rubbing his face)
What the heck is wrong with you? Tom boy!

He darts off... Jasmine chases after him... Candace goes back to watching the tube.

INT. HOUSE PARTY, LIVING ROOM - CONTINUOUS: LOUD RAP music. Different TEENAGE BOYS and TEENAGE GIRLS talking and dancing. Jasmine DRUNKENLY dances in the middle of a cluster of TEEN AGE BOYS as they loudly and cheerily pour beers down her shirt. Everyone goes nuts. Candace stands alone watching Jasmine.

CANDACE
What's the point of this?

EXT. CANDACE'S HOUSE - CONTINUOUS: Jasmine's station wagon pulls up in front of Candace's house. Candace gets out, makes her way to the front door. Jasmine's station wagon pulls off. Candace enters her bedroom, sits on the bed, bothered.

Chad enters the bedroom. Candace looks at him.

CHAD
How did everything go at the party tonight?

CANDACE
I pretty much cornered myself into a room and watched sports center the whole time I was there.

CHAD (cheerful)
Really? That's wonderful!

CANDACE
There were a ton of guys there.

                              CHAD

There was? Did any of them — try anything
foolish?

Candace is embarrassed.

CHAD sighs.

                         CHAD (cont'd)

Please tell me you didn't, gosh dam it.

                      CHANDACE (offended)

Nothing happened dad.

She gets up, moves away from Chad. Chad comes up from behind.

                         CHAD (cont'd)

I'm sorry — it's just that your mother and I were
worried sick about you being out past curfew.

                             CANDACE

Dad, I'm not a kid anymore.

Jane enters. Chad gestures — "Not now!" Jane quickly exits.

                              CHAD

Okay, from here on out your mother and I will
give you your space, I'm sorry.

He hugs her. He exits the bedroom.

INT. CONVENIENT STORE - EVENING: Candace motions down
the ale. She SCANS the shelves for tampons. Uncertain, she grabs the most
colorful box of tampons she sees. She picks out a pair of gold-plated studded
earrings in the jewelry sections of the store. She walks up to the counter to pay
for the tampons and earrings. She tosses the box of tampons on the counter.

She gently sets the earrings on the counter. A TEENAGE BOY CLERK stands behind the cash register. He GRABS and STARES at the box of tampons.

The moment is awkward.

TEENAGE BOY CLERK
Cool! So did you find everything okay miss?

She quickly tosses a ten dollar bill on the counter. She SNATCHES the tampons and earrings and quickly exits the store.

TEENAGE BOY CLERK (cont'd)
Miss you forgot your change.

INT. BEDROOM - CONTINUOUS: Terrence stands in front of dresser mirror fixing his tie, wears a black dapper three piece suite. Tina comes up from behind in a sexy red dress. She reaches her arms around his neck and helps him with his tie.

TINA
You are gonna knock them dead tonight Mr. smooth dark and handsome.

He turns to face her. Looks her up and down.

TERRENCE
You're wearing my favorite dress tonight.

He leans in.. smells her neck.

TERRENCE (cont'd)
Umm, and my favorite perfume.

He smooches her neck, she playfully pulls away.

TINA
Save it for the after party, Tarzan.

He grabs her hand, they exit the bedroom.

INT. TINA'S SEDAN: They pull up in front of Candace's house. We hear music coming from inside the house. Cars are parked in the driveway and across the lawn. Tina looks at Terrence.

TINA (cont'd)

Well, here we are, looks like they started without us.

TERRENCE (looks through window)

You're right about that, we better head on in.

He gets out of the car first, moves over to driver side and opens the door for Tina. Tina emerges, they move up to the front door. Terrence knocks on the door hard.

Both Chad and Jane appear.

TERRENCE AND TINA (excitedly)

Surprise!

CHAD

Hey guys glad you could make it.

TERRENCE

This is my fiancé, Tina.

JANE

Well don't you look stunning!

TINA

Why thank you, I love your necklace!

JANE

Chad got it for me on our fifth anniversary.

They hug.

CHAD

Terrence, you never tell me you were engaged to a super model.

TERRENCE

Tina, I'd like for you to meet part of my second family.

TINA (To Chad and Jane)

The pleasures all mine.

JANE (To Terrence and Tina)

Come inside...

They all enter.

EXT. CANDACE'S BEDROOM- CONTINUOUS: Candace stands in front of her dresser mirror putting on the gold studded earrings. She is wearing grey ish evening gown and make up, her hair is done up nice.

ENT. LIVING ROOM -CONTINUOUS: Different people standing and sitting on the couch talking. Tina and Jane are off in the corner talking.

Terrence stands next to Chad, they hold brews.

TERRENCE

So what do you think about, Tina? Amazing isn't she?

CHAD

You are one lucky man...

TERRENCE

She wont let me forget it, hard to believe we started out as high school sweethearts.

                              CHAD

Nooo way, you guys have been dating since high
school?

                            TERRENCE

Yes sir, we were a pair of wild and crazy love birds,
our plan was simple. I get drafted into the NBA.
and she pursue her passion for art.

They clank bottles.

                              CHAD

Here's to a long and prosperous relationship!

They drink.

Candace enters the living room. Terrence sees her first.

                            TERRENCE

Ahhh, the women of the hour. I'm gonna go over
and say hello.

He moves over to her...Tina and Jane stand next to windowsill. Jane caresses
Tina's face.

                              JANE

Your skin is so flawless you just have to tell me
what skin cream your using.

She sticks out her engagement ring on her finger.

                              TINA

This is what's causing it.

Jane grabs her hand, studies her ring.

                              JANE

That is absolutely gorgeous.

TINA
Thank you, he says he's been saving up to buy me a ring ever since we were juniors in high school— so he says.

Jane exhales to show her emotions. Candace and Terrence stand next to punch bowl. He hands her a glass of punch.

CANDACE
Wow, you weren't kidding about me not having any alcohol were you.

TERRENCE
Now what kind of mentor would I be to you if I were to let you tilt back a couple?

She looks around, then leans in..

CANDACE
A very cool one.

He chugs his brew.

TERRENCE
So, how did it go at Jasmine's party?

CANDACE
Oh, well, it went.

TERRENCE
Did any guys ask you out on a date?

CANDACE
A few, but, none of them interest me. However, there was this one guy who wouldn't take no for an answer, so I kindly blew him off.

He stares at her.

CANDACE (cont'd)

In a vicious sort of way.

TERRENCE

That's good to hear because you really shouldn't be dating until you're done with college.

She smacks him on his shoulder.

TERRENCE (cont'd)

Okay I take that back..

She glances at Tina and Jane talking.

CANDACE

Who's the hot babe over there talking to my mom?

TERRENCE

That would be Tina, my finance. And I think it's time you both met.

He grabs her arm, and they motion over towards Tina and Jane. They walk to Tina and Jane.

TERRENCE (cont'd)

Tina, this is Candace. Candace just happens to be my promising protégé.

TINA

So this is the person you've been talking about so much. Candace, its very nice to meet you, finally.

She clasps her hand.

CANDACE

It's nice to meet you also.

TERRENCE (To Tina)

Candace made the dean's list this year.

TINA

Oh wow, congrats. We diffidently have to sit down and have ourselves a dean's honoree to deans honoree chat.

TERRENCE

When were in high school Tina made the dean's list four straight years in a row and finished off her undergrad at Yale University.

Tina is blushing.

JANE

Wooo hoo!

CANDACE

Man, that must have been hard.

TINA

Well, it was actually a lot easier than you think, like I always say, geeks rule!

She raises up both hands and makes a famous frat club gesture. Candace frowns.

TINA (cont'd)

Don't mind me...

This would be when, we hear a dinner bell RINGING. Chad stands in the center of the living room holding a wine glass over his head as he prepares to make a toast.

CHAD

May I have everyone's attention please!

Everyone turns to him.

> ### CHAD (cont'd)
> Hello everyone! For those of you who don't know
> who I am, I'm the guy who helped out with the
> party decorations.

They all laugh and have a look around.

> ### CHAD (cont'd)
> I'll keep this short and sweet. A good friend
> of mine, oh hell, A person who I've grown to
> respect and appreciate over the years and has
> been somewhat of a big brother to my daughter
> Candace —whether he know it or not, is here to
> night, and I'd like for him to come up here and say
> a few words, that's if he not shy.

Everyone laughs….. Chad gestures Terrence to come over to him, Terrence
tries to avoid eye contact. Tina pushes him to the center of the room next to
Chad and walks back over to Jane and Candace.

> ### TERRENCE (To Chad)
> So much for no surprises.

Everyone laughs.

> ### CHAD
> Go ahead and say a few words, your getting
> married in a couple of month for Christ Sake.

Chad backs away. Terrence just stands there. Then:

> ### TERRENCE (exhales, nervously)
> Well, yeah, I'm not really good at giving speeches,
> so I'll make this short and sweet as Chad was
> saying.

He glances at Chad. He looks at Tina.

TERRENCE (cont'd)
I've been very fortunate to have good support and good people around me. My father use to tell me that it takes a village to raise a child and despite the fact that he up and left me at the age of eighteen doesn't change the fact that— til this day I hold every bit of his advise very close to me.

He looks at Tina.

TERRENCE (cont'd)
If there is anyone here tonight who don't believe in miracles, I'd say to you that person, give love a try.

Tina is blushing and teary eyed.

TERRENCE (cont'd)
Tina, you mean the world to me in every aspect.

She pulls back tears.

TERRENCE (cont'd)
The first day I laid eyes on you I knew you were the one for me.

She starts to cry. Candace hands her a napkin to wipe her tears. Chad walks up to him and puts his arm around him.

Just then, we hear a knock on the door. Everyone turns to the door.

CANDACE
I'll get it!

Candace moves over to the door. She opens the door.

Coach Mayday appears with two TALL AFRICAN AMERICAN JOCKS.

Candace's mouth drops wide open.

CANDACE
Coach Mayday, what are you doing here?

COACH MAYDAY
Now, Candace, is that any way to treat your ex basketball coach.

CANDACE
How did you get my address?

He pushes her aside, she falls down to the ground, they all enter. Terrence frowns anger. Candace is pissed. Terrence has to hold himself back from clocking coach Mayday.

COACH MAYDAY
Carry on everyone, carry on.

Everyone looks around confused. Jane moves over by Chad.

JANE (To Chad)
I'm calling the police.

Terrence walks up to Chad and Jane.

TERRENCE (To Chad and Jane)
Let me handle this.

He moves over to them. Tina tries to stop him, he pushes her aside. Terrence walks up to coach Mayday.

TERRENCE (cont'd)
I don't know what you're doing here, but you were not invited, therefore I'm gonna have to ask you to leave the premises, ASAP.

The two jocks walk up to Terrence acting as coach Mayday's bodyguard.

JOCK #1
Coach don't need no invitation, shrimp.

Chad moves over to them.

CHAD
Alright-alright that's enough the police are on
their way so I suggest you guys get moving..

One of the jocks move in front of the telephone so that Jane cant call the cops.
Jane moves back over to Tina extremely frightened.

TERRENCE (To coach Mayday)
I'm giving you and your goones three seconds to
take off... or else...

COACH MAYDAY
You don't have the guts, boy.

TERRENCE (grows angry)
What did you just say to me?

COACH MAYDAY
I said you don't have the guts to make us walk out
of here, BOY!

TERRENCE
The last time a black man was called a boy was
when slavery was legal.

Terrence loses his temper. He glance at Tina. He stares at coach Mayday.

TERRENCE (cont'd)
If you think I'm just gonna stand here and let you
disrespect me in front my lady you got another
thing coming.

Coach Mayday pushes him backward.

TERRENCE (To Tina)
Did he just put his hands on me?

TINA (serious)
Terrence, no, I want you to take a deep breath and settle down. He's not worth it.

Terrence stares at her, pure rage. Tina sighs.

TINA (cont'd)
Terrence, I'm ready to go home.

COACH MAYDAY
You better listen to your lady unless you want to be carried out here on a stretcher.

TERRENCE (To coach Mayday)
You be quiet.

He looks at Tina.

TERRENCE (contd)
Baby, a man's gotta do what a man's gotta do.

TINA
If you lay one finger on him our marriage is off.

He is confused and pissed off.

TERRENCE
First this punk crashes the party and now you're letting him get in the way of us getting married? What the hell is going on with you?

TINA (mad)
This is not about him Terrence, this is about you controlling your anger and not getting involved in

a fist fight just to prove your manhood to me or anyone else in this room.

COACH MAYDAY
Wow, I guess that makes me your God, Terrence.

TINA
Terrence, do not listen to him.

Terrence is completely frustrated and confused on what to do. Coach Mayday stares at Tina. Coach Mayday tries to get a reaction out of him by provoking him even more.

COACH MAYDAY (Refers to Tina)
You sure do know how to pick'um, Terrence. She's a little on the bow legged side but just how I like'um.

Terrence snaps.

Just then.

Terrence punches him in the face. Pow! They start fist fighting in the middle of the living room. Everyone moves away..

TINA
I'm done.

She pulls her engagement ring off her finger and tosses it at Terrence as he gets punched in the face by coach Mayday.

She heads for the exit, crying.

Terrence and coach Mayday roll around on the ground throwing punches... Smack! Ping! Pop!

The two jocks step in and pull Terrence up off of coach Mayday. Coach Mayday spit out blood from his mouth.

COACH MAYDAY
This aint over...

They move towards the door. Terrence looks around for Tina, sees the engagement ring on the floor. He quickly picks it up and runs for the exit as he tries to stop Tina from leaving the party. Chad looks down at the ground, sad.

CHAD (exhales)
Oh damn.

EXT. CANDACE'S HOUSE-CONTINUOUS: Tina pulls off, Terrence chases after her...

TERRENCE
Tina! Tina! Wait! I'm sorry!

He continues to chase after her...

INT. CANDACE'S HOUSE-CONTINUOUS: CANDACE stands next to CHAD as she watches coach Mayday and his jocks walk out the door.

CANDACE (serious)
I'll pay you for it, settle the score once and for all. My team against yours. You can be the coach of your team and Terrence will be the coach of my team.

COACH MAYDAY
The only way I would even consider playing your team is if you put that coach of yours on a leash.

She stares...

COACH MAYDAY (cont'd)
To reassure that none of my players get injured.

CANDACE (nods)
Okay.

Coach Mayday looks at his players then looks at Candace.

COACH MAYDAY

There's a 5 on 5 tournament going on at the playground in about a another month, you have your team down there ready to play.

She nods. They exit. She looks at both Chad and Jane.

CANDACE (excited)

I gotta go find Terrence to tell him the good news.

She exits...

EXT. TINA'S APARTMENT- CONTINUOUS: Terrence stands at the front door, knocking hard.

TERRENCE

Tina, I made a mistake, please open the door.

He falls down next to door, starts crying. Tina half-opens the door. He rushes up and stares at her.

TERRENCE (cont'd)(teary eyed)

Baby, I'm sorry, I'll do whatever you want me to do to make us whole again.

She stares at him..

TERRENCE (cont'd)

I know I have anger management problem and I'm willing to get help, I promise you.

Just then Tina's friend walks up to them, Terrence looks confused.

SAMANTHA (To Tina)

Can we go?

TERRENCE (To Samantha)

Go where? Where are you taking my fiance?

SAMANTHA (serious) (To Terrence)

She's not your fiance anymore.

Tina opens the door, stares at Terrence.

TINA

Terrence, that little stunt you pulled tonight made it very clear to me that you'd rather break some guys face than listen to your girl who took you in when you were piss-poor and had nowhere to go.

TERRENCE (cry's harder)

Tina, you don't mean that, I understand you're a little upset right now —that guy at the party hand it in for me the whole time he was there.

SAMANTHA

Girl friend you can do a lot better then this loser.

He stares at her, pathetic. She stares at him.

TINA

I can't do this anymore.

Samantha puts her arm around her to comfort her.

TERRENCE (crying)

I never meant for any of this to happen.

They walk off.. still laying on the ground Terrence desperately grabs one of Tina's legs...

TERRENCE (cont'd)

Tina, don't leave.

Samantha quickly kicks him off of her, he falls to the ground, tries to get back up, Samantha stands over him, pins him down with her bare hand.

> ### SAMANTHA angry) (To Terrence)
> Try that again and I will break you in half.

She pushes him to the ground again, They walk off and leave him there on the ground.

INT. CANDACE'S HOUSE LIVING ROOM -CONTINUOUS: Jane and Chad stand at the door as they watch different guest leaving the party. A TEENAGE BOY walk up to Chad.

> ### TEENAGE BOY (excited)
> Cool party Mr. Fukumi. Action packed! Yeaaah!

He walks off.

Chad and Jane look around.

> ### CHAD AND JANE
> Candace!!!

> ### JANE
> You pull the car around. I'll grab Melissa and our coats.

They quickly move in the house and shut the door.

EXT. SIDEWALK — CONTINUOUS: Terrence motions down the sidewalk, piss poor, and feeling hopeless.

EXT. STREET — CONTINUOUS: Candace runs down the street in between parked cars yelling out Terrence's name.

> ### CANDACE
> Terrence! I got us game!

She looks around.

CANDACE (cont'd)

Now if I could just find you.

She approaches the basketball courts. It's empty. She knells down, fatigued. Shortly after: Chad's SUV pulls up to her.

CHAD

Any luck?

Candace still knelling down, shakes her head, no.

CHAD signs.

CHAD

Get in the car.

CANDACE (sad)

I didn't get chance to tell him.

She unhappily gets inside of the car. They pull off.

EXT. BANK -CONTINUOUS: Terrence sits in front of the bank, extremely sad.

EXT. CAR WASH - MORNING: Terrence and TWO MIDDLE AGED MEN stand next to each other aggressively HAND WASHING a red sedan. Terrence is wearing a rubber suit, gloves, and rubber boots.

INT. GYM, BASKETBALL COURT - MORNING: Coach Mayday monitors TWO TEENAGE JOCKS as they work on lay-ups. A JOCK walks up to him. He hands him a note — a bet from both Candace and Chad.

He reads the note.

"One hundred grand." Are they serious? Who bets one hundred grand on a basketball game?

JOCK

His childhood friend has deep pockets. It will be like taking candy from a baby.

THEY LAUGH.

"ONE WEEK LATER"

INT. CANDACE'S BEDROOM - LATE AFTERNOON: Candace PLOWS down hard on the bed in her bedroom drenched in sweat and extremely fatigued.

She wears sports attire. Jane enters her room.

JANE

How was basketball practice?

Candace gestures: "Great!"

JANE (cont'd)

Well if it makes you feel any better, your father was able to get in touch with Terrence, he found him sleeping underneath a freeway overpass.

She exits the room. Candace quickly raises up, unsure..

"THREE DAYS LATER"

EXT. BASKETBALL COURTS - DAY: Terrence stands at the sideline watching hang time and coach Mayday's team warm-up. He wears a worn three piece suit. He gestures for the hang time team to come over to him. Hang time's uniforms are white with gold trim, printed on the uniform is the words: HANG TIME. CANDACE and the players walk up to him. He sees Carl sitting to his left and Mr. Santana sitting to his right as they both wait for the game to start.

CANDACE
I hope you don't mind that I invited a couple of your old pals.

He still looks nervous.

CANDACE (cont'd)(to Terrence)
So what's the game plan?

Terrence glances at coach Mayday. He looks at Candace.

TERRENCE
We will show them no mercy.

Everyone leans in.

CANDACE (loudly)
Whose house is this?!

HANG TIME TEAMMATES (loudly)
Hang time! Woo!

Coach Mayday CLAPS Terrence over his shoulder.

COACH MAYDAY
May the best man win.

On the court the referee TOSSES UP the basketball.

A HANG TIME PLAYER SKIES up for the tip against the OPPOSING TEAM FORWARD.

Second quarter. Fifty-three seconds left. Hang time down six.

TERRENCE (shots)

Isolation for, Candace!

On the court, CANDACE does dancy dribbling in front of a MALE JOCK.

MALE JOCK (trash talking)

Show me what you got short-stuff!

She makes a timely move pass the MALE JOCK and scores a lay-up. coach Mayday is upset!

COACH MAYDAY (shouts)

Jezzzzz! Guard her!

On the court, all the MALE JOCKS run over to their bench as hang time slowly moves to their bench, fatigued and battered.

EXT. SIDEWALK — CONTINUOUS: Tina and Samantha move down the sidewalk as they head to the nail shop. Tina glances at Terrence from afar.

TINA

Is that my ex over there on the basketball courts.

She stops, takes a closer look.

TINA (contd)

Terrence?

SAMANTHA

Tina, the nail shop is just a few blocks up the street so we really don't have any extra time to waste, besides, I thought you were over him.

Tina stares at him.

TINA

He went and got his act together just like he promised.

Samantha sighs.

                        TINA (cont'd)
I'm gonna go watch a little bit of the game, I'll
meet you at the nail shop later.

Samantha sighs again, storms off, Tina moves over to the courts.

EXT. BASKETBALL COURTS — CONTINUOUS

            TERRENCE (to hang time team members)
We have to do a much better job of keeping their
big men off the glass.

Terrence looks at CANDACE, pulls everyone in a huddle.

                TERRENCE (cont'd) (loudly)
On three, One! Two! Three!

                HANG TIME TEAMMATES (shouts)
Hang Time!

On the court, CANDACE throws up a shot. Swish!

On the court, A MALE JOCK scores a lay-up.

On the court, CANDACE scores back-to-back three pointers. Third quarter.
One minute left. Hang Time down five.

                        TERRENCE
Pass and cut! Move! Move!

On the court, CANDACE passes the ball to a WIDE-OPEN teammate. The
teammate dribble-drives in for a lay-up. The shot is BLOCKED BY TWO
MALE JOCKS. Terrence goes nuts! He calls a time out!

Fourth quarter. Two minutes left. Hang Time down two.

On the court, TWO MALE JOCKS intentionally SHOVE CANDACE to the floor. CANDACE is slow to get up, grabs her knee –- winches in pain. She walks with a noticeable limp toward the bench. Terrence YELLS at the referee.

> ### TERRENCE (cont'd) (shouts)
> Hey ref, what game are you watching out there?!

Chad raises up in the stands.

> ### CHAD (shouts)
> Call it both ways ref!

> ### TERRENCE (shouts.) (gestures to referee)
> Time out!

> ### REFEREE (shouts)
> Time out white!

On the court, all of the HANG TIME TEAM MEMBERS are beaten down. They slowly head over to their bench. CANDACE LIMPS over to the bench and sits down. Terrence looks at her.

> ### TERRENCE
> I'm setting you up for the win.

CANDACE –- looking down, extremely fatigued, nods. The referee walks over to hang time's bench.

> ### REFEREE (To Terrence)
> You have no more timeouts left coach, your ball
> at the half court.

He walks away. Terrence looks over at coach Mayday's bench as he yells at his team to regain their focus. Terrence NERVOUSLY looks at the scoreboard.

THREE SECONDS LEFT IN THE FOURTH QUARTER. HANGTIME DOWN TWO. He sees Tina, he lights up, she blows him a kiss for good luck. He looks at everyone:

TERRENCE

Stella and Kendall, I want you two to set a double screen for Candace, Candace as soon as Stella and Kendall are in position I want you to come off the block hard for an open look behind the arch. Cindy will be in charge of inbounding the basketball. Let's get a win!

Everyone CLAPS their hands together in the huddle.

TERRENCE (cont'd)

Win-on-three, One! Two! Three!

HANG TIME TEAMMATES (shouts)

Win!

On the court, Cindy stands out of bounds clutching the basketball. The REFEREE BLOWS his whistle to start the game. Stella and Kendall QUICKLY run over to Candace, Candace BAITS her DEFENDER right, QUICKLY moves left pass Stella and Kendall.

Candace is WIDE-OPEN. Cindy PASSES the ball to Candace.

Game on the line. Candace CATCHES the ball, turns to face the hoop, looks at Terrence.

Candace's point of view –- Terrence stands in **FULL COLOR**. She shoots the ball with one second remaining on the game clock.

Terrence watches the ball as it travels IN THE AIR. He is hopeful. Coach Mayday nervously watch the ball. Chad, Jane, Melissa, Mr. Santana, and Carl stare wide eyed. Tina nervously covers her eyes with both her hands.

Basketball SWOOSHES THOUGH NET!

Terrence falls to the ground in disbelief and excited.

Candace and the entire hang time team members are celebrating in the background.

Chad, Jane, Melissa, Mr. Santana, and Carl all give each other high fives, excitingly.

Tina runs up to Terrence, he gets up.

TINA

That was truly awesome....

Terrence sighs relief.

TINA

So, I was thinking that if you're not doing anything after the game... that... maybe we can grab a cappuccino at our favorite spot.

TERRENCE

I'd like that.

She gives him a big kiss and a warm hug.

Chad, Jane, Melissa, Mr. Santana, and Carl walk up to him, cheering and celebrating.

MR SANTANA

I always knew you were a team player, Terrence!

TERRENCE

Thanks for coming out...

MR SANTANA

I wouldn't miss it for the world.

Candace and Terrence high five each other as they both have accomplished their biggest milestone, together.

INT. TERRENCE'S APARTMENT — DAY: A series of welcome home banners pinned up throughout the living room that reads: "WELCOME HOME HARRISON AND LYNN". Terrence sits across from Harrison and Lynn as they hug each other.

TERRENCE

You guys deserve each other.

Terrence receives an incoming text from Chad.

He looks up at Harrison and Lynn — still hugging them both.

TERRENCE (cont'd)
Can you too hang tight? I gotta go take care of
something really quick.

Terrence takes off running...

EXT. BASKETBALL COURTS — CONTINUOUS: Terrence arrives
at the courts and walks up to Candace, she wears a U.S.C. sweat suit. She is
standing next to Chad, Jane, and Melissa as they all watch different players on
the basketball court in an intense game of five on five.

Candace hands Terrence a secret note.

The secret note reads: (16) FUKUMI (PROTÉGÉ): **COLOR BLIND.**

He looks at the different players on the court, they are in a silhouette. Candace
looks at Terrence and he stands in FULL COLOR.

He becomes teary eyed.

                    CANDACE
You see Terrence, I fixed you....can you see them?

Teary eyed. He happily nods...

                    TERRENCE
Yes, I can see them.... your special talent stems
far beyond the game of basketball.

Candace stares out...

                    TERRENCE
As a man, I'm not ashamed to admit that this
whole thing was never about me giving up on
you... it was about you never giving up on me...
And by-the-way...... congratulations on your
basketball scholarship to U.S.C..

CANDACE

I couldn't of done it without you.

They turn to face the city, they both see different silhouettes moving throughout the city....

CANDACE (cont'd)

The world isn't so bad after all.

TERRENCE

Agreed.

They look at the city.

THE END

ABOUT THE AUTHOR

Tony Hood, started out his basketball showmanship at the tender age of eleven.

Tony's passion for the game of basketball took flight one summer afternoon, at the Magic Johnson's basketball camp awards ceremony.

Tony was also just eleven years of age when he received his life changing award as Magic Johnson's basketball camp's Premiere Play Maker.

From that point, Tony played in numerous basketball ball Amateur Athletic sporting events in which he honed his basketball skills, which later in life, helped him obtain a basketball scholarship to help him pay his way through college.

Eventually, Tony would take on the roll of mentoring and coaching kids, of all ages, as he developed a passion for teaching the game of basketball, as much as he loved to play the game of basketball.

One can say that, over the many years of playing under the tutelage of tough, hard nosed, and gritty basketball personalities, and becoming a student of the game, this was ultimately what help propel Tony's venture into both the basketball mentoring and basketball coaching world.

I believe readers will be interested in reading material by Tony Hood, as this particular piece, symbolizes the bare essence of how sports crosses all types of racial barriers in reference to building a team atmosphere to achieve the ultimate goal, which is none other than, winning.

Tony Hood's writing capacity shows both an in dept look and understanding of how kids are able to move up through the ranks of someday obtaining either, a basketball scholarship, or, landing a career as a professional basketball sports figure, in this case, becoming a sought after basketball, blue chipper.

Race in this case, has never played a major role in a team atmosphere of the basketball world, or any sport for that matter, as each member of a team, whether it be: basketball, football, soccer, baseball etc.

Will find a way to work together, and make plays together, blood, sweat, and tears together, as a collective effort, to bring home the victory.

Tony Hood, has found a way to deliver a basketball story, that, identifies race relations and gender relations in the sport of basketball, whereas, -- it seems as though there really isn't much race relations involved in obtaining the goal of out performing the opponent or the competition.

Additionally, Tony Hood, identifies the important role of the unsung hero who plays an important role in both mentoring and helping propel each student athletes's career forward.

These special individuals [unsung hero's] usually work behind the scenes in honing each individual basketball player's: skill sets, conditioning, and more importantly, helping them develop a great attitude which ultimately sets each individual student-athlete up for success.

To sum it up, this book, gives a wonderful in site on both: how race relations and gender relations work diligently together with one simple goal in mind which is none other than winning against stiff competition.

And giving our unsung hero's in the basketball, training and coaching world some well deserved credit. Perhaps.

Printed in the United States
By Bookmasters